Broken Wings

AN ADVENTURE IN FOSTER CARE

Andela Jamison

WESTBOW
PRESS
A DIVISION OF THOMAS NELSON
& ZONDERVAN

WestBow Press books may be ordered through booksellers or by contacting:

WestBow Press
A Division of Thomas Nelson & Zondervan
1663 Liberty Drive
Bloomington, IN 47403
www.westbowpress.com
1 (866) 928-1240

ISBN: 978-1-4908-8519-3 (sc)
ISBN: 978-1-4908-8520-9 (e)

Library of Congress Control Number: 2015909816

Print information available on the last page.

WestBow Press rev. date: 10/27/2015

Contents

Dedication

For my mom, who taught me the true value of a child.
Thank you for instilling this in me.
I surely miss you.

Acknowledgments

To my wonderful husband, pastor and best friend: Thank you for more than thirty-eight years of love and faithful companionship. You are my strength and source of encouragement, without whom I would be lost. You are a godly man and a true father to the fatherless. I adore you.

To our older children: thank you for sharing your parents with the many children over the years who needed a family.

To Their spouses: Thank you for the beautiful grandchildren and allowing them to share their "Nana and Pappy" as well.

To our eight adopted children: Thank you for the privilege of being called "Mom and Dad"

To all the foster children who have come and gone (deep sigh): Thank you for letting us love you.

To Elizabeth Witt: Thank you for your encouragement and keen editorial skills.

Most of all, to my heavenly father: Thank you for calling me to care for hurting children everywhere and for equipping me with the love and patience I need every day.

Introduction

"Please, God, take this burden away! I cannot handle this pain! Why can't we keep just one?"

I sobbed uncontrollably, as I lay across our king-sized bed. We had just returned from the courthouse, where it had been ordered that the little guy we had come to love over the last two years was to be returned to his biological father and stepmother. The words of the Juvenile Master had pricked my heart like a thorn. He had stated,

"Common sense would be to leave the child with the Jamison's, but I'm going to rule the child be returned to his biological family immediately."

We had a couple of months to pack the last two years of this little boy's life into a few cardboard boxes.

The sorrow was more than I could bear. I counted the cost of caring and found my own account overdrawn. My heart was torn into more pieces than I even knew had existed. I thought, "Never again will I be so foolish as to love so passionately! Never again will I let myself give without receiving!"

I had grown to believe that it was the Lord's will for us to adopt this little boy named Jacob. How could this have turned around so profoundly? I was more than angry. After all, by faith, I purchased a children's bible and had his full adoptive name engraved on the cover. I truly believed he was meant to stay and be our son.

More than fifty children had passed through our doors by that time. We always knew they were not our children, and that one day they would be returned to their families, where they belonged. Still, my heart would not be consoled. At this crucial point, I decided to stop being a foster parent. I wanted nothing more than to be released from this love I have for children. It simply hurt too much. Child after child had entered into our home wounded and broken. We happily bound their wounds, and loved them like our own. They left us with holes inside that would forever remain empty. I felt this last heartbreaking event was my proverbial last straw.

Of course it wasn't. Over the years, we cared for so many more children who needed us. We picked them up in emergency rooms, police stations, and courthouses. They came wearing anything from a stiff t-shirt covered with three days of play to a urine-soaked sleeper with a two day old diaper drooping down one leg.

All of the children who passed through our lives were angels, angels with broken wings. Most of the parents had been charged with abuse, neglect, or child endangerment. They came at any hour, day or night. The phone would ring, the proper car seat would be loaded into the car, and off we would bound to collect another angel. We would gather the precious bundles and set out to repair the broken wings. The angels appeared and stayed for hours, week, or even years. They came empty-handed, stealing pieces of our hearts as they passed through our lives.

These are the stories of some of the many angels who have entered our hearts and lives for a brief time. It is my desire to touch your hearts as the angels have touched ours.

Jacob

Twenty years have passed since we took the call that we thought led to our greatest heartbreak. It turns out, this was only the beginning. My husband, Jake, had taken our daughter with him on his mission to collect and angel. As I paced and peered out the window, waiting anxiously for their return, I wondered what we would need to help this little one with. I was in the kitchen when I heard the front door open. My daughter held a two-year-old, button-eyed boy, tightly in her arms. As I laughed at his inquisitive expressions, I did not hear my husband call my name.

Little Jacob had delightful, coal black eyes that sparkled with the radiance of a diamond. He was fidgety and looked scared to death. His little eyes flashed as they took in the living room. If the little guy had been bidding for my heart, the auctioneer would have surely announced, "Sold!" As I blinked away a tear of bliss, I heard a noise behind me. As I turned toward the sound, I was thrilled to find an infant in a small car seat.

"Surprise!" Jake blurted. We didn't know he had a baby brother.

I promptly loosened the straps of the seat, gathered up the small bundle and delivered him from his snowsuit. His blue, knit hat popped off, revealing his little, bald head.

"He looks like a miniature old man!" I laughed as I picked him up and planted a kiss on his shiny top.

This little tyke named Joey was a blue-eyed treasure. At five months, he was noticeably behind developmentally. He lay still as a newborn and did not attempt to reach for toys, his fingers or a bottle. He did not like to sit upright, and was frightened by sudden movements. Oh, but he could smile! His little toothless grins caused frequent outbursts of laughter.

After some time passed, and with the undivided attention he began to receive from our twin daughters, it seemed his "lights" turned on. Joey was captivated by everything. In the months that passed by ever so quickly, he became interested in playing, crawling, and eventually walking. Every day marked another milestone in his life; and before long, he was involved in his brother's mischief.

We learned that the little brothers could be quite a handful. It was fun having two little boys to look after, or should I say, chase after. Jacob was very busy. His daredevil feats were hidden from me. I thought everyone else exaggerated his waywardness. In my presence, he was a perfect angel. I was often told of the death-defying deeds performed by this little acrobat in my absence. I was becoming frustrated and could not believe what I was hearing. It was reported that he would run across the backs of the living room furniture, swing on the lights over the dining room table and hurl countless objects into the ceiling fan. However, as soon as I would enter the room, his little horns would disappear and he would sprout a tiny halo, transforming him back into the sweet cherub I knew.

One day, my husband convinced me to sneak up on Jacob to see what he was really up to. I crept down the basement steps and slipped out the door to our backyard. I turned the corner and quietly peered into the living room window. I was mortified by the sight of Jacob attempting to climb up the coat closet to retrieve a small basketball from the shelf. This was the very same ball that had been stashed there, after it sailed across the room, hitting the ceiling fan only minutes before. All this action took place in the time it took me to sneak up on him. I surrendered!

After several months of counseling, we came to understand that Jacob's "perfection" was solely for my benefit. Deep inside, his self-esteem barely existed. His spirit had been crushed by the confusion of having been abused by the only person he knew he could trust, his mother.

Jacob was driven by his need for approval. He would select one person to be loyal to and to please. This happened to be me. As long as he had me fooled in to believing he was the perfect angel, he was comfortable to act out around others. He cared very little of anyone else's opinion of him or his behaviors. Play therapy with a qualified therapist helped uncover some of his frustrations. After many sessions and a truckload of exhausting love and patience, the true Jacob was revealed. He became more disobedient to me, which actually was good thing. He sure was a rowdy little boy.

Jacob was diagnosed with A.D.H.D. (Attention Deficit Hyperactive Disorder), which was treatable with the right medications. We chose to wait until we were more educated before medicating him and, on the advice of his therapist, due to his young age. He had so many things going on with him that they did not want to risk misdiagnosing him or masking any underlying symptoms.

As the months passed, it was wonderful to see Jacob finally acting the same way toward everyone in the household. He began transforming from an intolerable tyrant, into a lovable, somewhat controlled child. He had a special way of lighting up a room. His presence demanded attention. His eyes were always full of stories. These were the kind of tales that caused you to applaud the narrator. His imagination was as wild as a stallion. It was a true gift.

We attended a hearing every six months to determine the boy's continued placement. This was normal for foster care. Most times we could sense what was coming. We did not see it coming, however when we were informed that Joey's biological father had obtained legal services and asked for his son to be given to him for full custody. Since the boys had different fathers, Jacob would stay with us another six months, and Joey would go with his father.

One month later, just before his second birthday, Joey left us to live with his dad. His dad was a young man, who was a hard worker with a good job. He had his own place where he lives with his fiancé. It was hard to see the boys separated, but it was nice to see how well Joey adjusted to being with his dad. To be honest, it calmed things down at our house. Jacob was able to visit with his brother several times over the following year or so, then they suddenly stopped coming around.

Jacob had lived with us long enough for the agency to start planning a permanency hearing so that we might be able to adopt him. At his permanency hearing, it was determined that since his mother had been charged with various crimes against children, she would not even be considered for custody. Jacob's father and stepmother were at the hearing. As our caseworker testified to Jacob's well-being in his present placement with our family, I felt certain that everything was going in favor of adoption. Suddenly, Jacob's father took the stand. He stated that even though he had not been a part of his son's life in the past, he wanted to have a chance to make up for lost time. He admitted to having made mistakes in the past but, was sure he, his new wife and their newborn son needed Jacob in their life. After his brief and apparently convincing testimonial, his lawyer demanded that the now six-year-old Jacob, be given to his father.

As the law permitted, foster parents could choose to testify in permanency hearings. I desperately took the stand and smiled, as I shared stories of Jacob's progress over the past four years. I told of my dreams of one day adopting him and providing him with a stable childhood. I expounded on my fears that everything was moving too quickly and that I did not agree that it would be in Jacob's best interest to go live with someone he barely knew. I was thanked for my words and promptly dismissed. The conclusion of the hearing was unmerciful; and with the cruel tap of the gavel, we were ordered to give Jacob to his father in two months. This would be just before Christmas.

The tears flowed hot as I clambered toward the door. It was impossible to make contact with the one who had just determined our fate as well as the fate of an innocent child who did not know his father. My teary-eyed husband gently led me down the hall toward the elevator. The doors were closed, blocking my escape. I stood sobbing as the doors opened. Inside my hand was the small, sympathetic hand of my now former son. I quickly looked away from the little face that was soaked with our pain. The thirty-minute drive home was interrupted only by the occasional sniff. There simply were no words.

I was determined not to deal with this major disappointment until after the holidays ended. I tried the "I'll think about that tomorrow," tenacity of Scarlett O'Hara. It was, of course, unsuccessful. Our sorrow dangled like the tinsel on the Christmas tree.

Two days before Christmas, when it really hit, I found myself sprawled across the gift wrap covered bed, sobbing inconsolably. How can we give up Jacob? It had only been five months since we decided to change his middle name to add to our last name which, we thought, would also become his. I had so many times scribbled his new name on scraps of paper, dinner napkins, and the frost on the window. I had it engraved on the front of his new bible I had purchased for him as a Christmas gift. Recalling this fact, I became enraged and scampered to my feet. I located the bible and hurled it across the room. It was as if my dreams had been slammed against a cold, hard wall. I quickly re-claimed the bible and held it close to my heart, and returned to my grief. I was angry at God and needed a nap.

Hours later, I woke up to the sweet aroma of fresh baked cookies. My husband thought, perhaps, it would cheer everyone up. He was right. It worked. After finishing off a plate of warm, sweet treats chased down by cold milk, we began gathering Jacobs' things. Together, Jake and I sorted through three years of toys, books and clothing. Jacob was to leave in the morning; Christmas Eve.

Once our blue van was packed, we headed down the dreary path to Jacob's future. Hot tears burned my face, as our brave, little man stared out the back window. Jake gazed ahead as he drove what felt like a hearse. This was the death of our plans.

We met Jacob's father at a shopping center parking lot. I stood by, clutching his little hand as his things went from the van to a rusty little pickup truck. It barely took a minute. The cold winter wind warmed in comparison to the blizzard inside my heart. The "good-byes" were quick as a bandage torn from a wound. It hurts no matter how fast you rip it.

We returned home in a flood of emotions. Christmas Day was nearly upon us, and we had a house full of family to enjoy. We welcomed the hustle and bustle of the holiday with our teen-age children. We smiled, laughed, and of course, ate too much. I knew the kids were feeling the loss as much as we were. I was so grateful for their support, and even though Christmas was a little less festive that year, I knew we would survive. It's what we do.

In the spring I decided to get on with mending wings. Over the next two years, we continued to bind up broken angel wings and send them on their way. There were no close encounters to lead to adoption, so things just continued as what we would consider normal, enjoying children along the way.

I decided to go to college. I thought, perhaps I could get a degree and open up a daycare. Maybe, just maybe I could give up being a foster parent then. It seemed safe enough. No more broken hearts for the Jamison clan.

For two years, I was a part-time student as well as a part-time employee of a local daycare. I went to school during the day and worked the evening shift at the daycare. Most of the days I attended classes, grabbed some fast food, and ate in my car until it was time for work. One day while picnicking in my car, I received a call from Jake.

"Honey?" my husband asked, "Do we want Jacob?"

I dropped my phone and began to sob. It had been awhile since he left. I had given up on him completely.

"Are you okay?" Jake asked as I returned the phone to my ear.

"I'm here, what's going on?"

"Well," he replied, "the county office called. They are removing Jacob from his home because things have gone badly. So, what do you think?"

"Call them and ask if this the real thing. I can't take losing him again. Tell them not to mess with my head. I can't go through it again!" I blurted to my husband.

A month passed without a word. We began to think that the previous conversation was premature. I was okay. I was busy with school and work. We had a teen mother and her infant living with us at the time, and I was quite content. We didn't talk about Jacob. But he never left our thoughts.

The call finally came. Jacob and his belongings could be collected in the morning. I began to cry as the caseworker informed me that Jacob's father signed papers relinquishing his parental rights. My curious husband was alerted by the tears. All I could do was signal "thumbs up," to which he responded with a deep sigh of relief.

The next morning, Jacob's eyes flashed as we entered the office of his caseworker to retrieve him. The eight-year-old jumped up from his chair and shouted,

"Yes! I knew it! I knew it!" he continued, "I told them I wanted to go back home with the Jamison's!" I didn't know then that I would someday regret his return.

Jacob chattered all the way to the parking garage. He paused momentarily to catch his breath, then continued to babble, telling story after story, about all the fights and nightmarish scenes that played out in his father's cabin. There were, according to Jacob, loud arguments that ended in cruel beatings inflicted on his stepmother, as well as he and his young half-brother.

On one occasion, which was confirmed to us later, the small boys were dragged into the woods where their drunken father threatened to shoot them, and then take his own life. Jacob said his father waved a pistol in his face and then dropped it. He then left the woods and turned himself in to the local police. That turned out to be the day that the county office had notified us a month earlier.

Jacob spent the last month with his biological grandmother and sickly grandfather. When they realized they could no longer provide care for him, they requested that Jacob be returned to us. We were more than happy to take him in, for keeps this time. We knew we had a long, uphill climb, but we held hands and started our ascent together, as a family.

The adoption was ironically finalized a few days before Christmas that year. In the courthouse, as we presented ourselves before the former Juvenile Master who had previously condemned our son to further abuse, I felt compelled to make a snide remark. Truth be told, I wanted to slap his face, but I sat silently, hoping that he had profoundly realized his near-fatal mistake. When all was said and done, we were given an opportunity to speak. I stood calm and firm. As a tear escaped down my cheek, I made eye contact with the Master, and with all the breath in my body, whispered,

"Thank you."

"Well spoken." came his meek reply.

I believe he knew my thoughts. Our brief past had finally ended, and now we were a family, anxious to try to repair the damage. There were fresh gashes on Jacob's wings that were in dire need of mending.

We had no clue to the extent of Jacob's emotional injuries. His bruised body healed with time, but the inner wounds ran deeper than anyone could imagine. We contacted his former therapist and began immediate counseling. Along with his previous diagnosis, he was given new and more frightening names for what now ailed him.

Attention Deficit Hyperactive Disorder, Post-Traumatic Stress Disorder, Anxiety Disorder with tendency to self-harm, and numerous social and learning disorders, hindered his relationship with his peers. Later, Attachment Disorder with mild suicidal tendencies was added to the list. Mild suicidal tendencies? Somehow, it all sounded serious. He was medicated, counseled and loved.

Jacob did well in elementary school, with support and special education. In middle school, however, he had a major meltdown. After a week-long stay in a mental health facility, and a six month battle with the school district, we were able to get approval for Jacob to attend a partial hospitalization program. This was a day school where he could be educated on his own learning level with the benefit of counsel, and with his medication being provided throughout the day.

For a while, everything seemed to be working out. However, Jacob began to sink. His behaviors became more erratic and life at home was beginning to be too stressful for everyone. Jacob was manipulative and untrustworthy, to say the least. He began a deep, downhill spiral, and began to fail in school.

After an unimaginable deep betrayal, and great hurt to our family, we had Jacob committed to yet another hospital. We had to protect ourselves, and the other children in our home, from further damage. We could not fix what was broken inside.

Jacob spent the next few years in various mental health facilities. His behavior escalated into harming himself, as he moved on to threaten others. He was finally placed in a group home where he could be better supervised. I visited him when I was emotionally able. No one in my family, other than my husband and one daughter, could bear to visit him. The pain was too deep.

On Jacob's eighteenth birthday, seven months before he was to graduate, his biological father and stepmother collected Jacob and his things. He had signed himself out of the facility, as was his right. He moved in with them and continued his behaviors.

His new behavior, over the last five years, is to move from girlfriend to girlfriend, fathering little ones along the way. We have had no contact with him since our last adventure concerning the welfare of three of his children, of which he has sole custody. It is in the best interest of our own mental health that we do not pursue any kind of relationship with him.

Sometimes there is just not enough chocolate.

Caitlyn

My husband and I tossed around the idea of becoming foster parents long before we took the plunge. We weighed out the pros and cons before abandoning our fears to jump in. If only I had a nickel for every time a friend or acquaintance commented our decision with, "Oh I would love to be a foster parent, but I would never be able to give them up."

Okay, so we are the kind of people that can toss out kids like the weekly trash. Actually, with some it was easy to do. For the most part, not so much. My mother used to say, "It's better to have loved and lost, than to never have loved." I think I understand that more now than ever.

Before my husband and I had finished our training with the county office, we received our first call. A young lady named Caitlyn, who was turning fifteen in a few days, was on her way to the women's center to have an abortion. We were asked to take care of her after, as a foster child. Before I could think, I agreed to take her as the caseworker abruptly ended the call. I was so caught off guard, I didn't have a chance to ask any questions. I cried. I wish I would have been given the opportunity to as the caseworker if there was any chance she could change her mind and allow us to adopt her baby. I sat stunned. There was little I could do at that point. My lack of experience left me feeling helpless. It was hours before the doorbell would finally ring. I anxiously awaited for the arrival of the child who would be our first of many.

Our own children agreed to share their parents with children in need. Originally we agreed to only take children under the age of ten, the age of our oldest son. We also had an eight-year-old son and six-year-old twin daughters. A teenager in the house would prove to be a real culture shock for us all.

Caitlyn arrived around eight-thirty that evening. She looked pale and untamed. Her long, curly locks draped over her right eye. She whispered a weak, "Hello," and made her way to the living room, as we obtained little information from her caseworker. We then hauled her belongings to her bedroom and gave her a quick tour of the house. Conversation was awkward, to say the least. We returned to her bedroom and asked if she needed anything before going to sleep. She asked for a glass of water to wash down a pain pill. After quietly collecting the empty glass, I paused at the closed bedroom door. I wondered what pain she carried inside that could not be dismissed with a pill.

In the months that followed, her body healed, but her spirit was crushed. She seemed to prefer a destructive path. She sneaked out on several occasions to run with her friend from school. We learned that when she said she was going to the library, that it meant she was going drinking. She was very promiscuous. She was failing from school and passing pregnancy tests. She lied. She put up all wall between us. She was unapproachable. We were out of our league.

One morning, as I struggled, once again, to get Caitlyn out of bed and off to school, she hid deep in her warm blankets and refused to acknowledge my urging. I began to lose my patience. It was our responsibility to see that she attended school. She was unmovable. I sat on the edge of her bed and talked. I talked about anything that popped into my head.

She turned in disgust at my constant babbling. I was certainly getting bored with myself. Still, I pressed on. I really wanted to push her to the brink. I held no degree in psychology, but felt that she needed to deal with her demons. I continued to rattle on and brought up the subject of her mother. Apparently, I struck a nerve. She cursed through the blankets. Too late to run.

"I hate her!" she screamed, startling me. "I gave up everything for her!"

Not completely sure what she meant, I pushed further.

"What in the world did you give up for her?" I asked.

"My babies!" She bolted upright in her bed.

I thought I had gone too far. My heart sank deep in my chest. What have I done?

"She hates my boyfriend," she sobbed. "I wanted to keep my baby the first time and she made me get rid of it. I hate her!"

"The first time?" I garbled. I had no idea until then that this had been her second abortion. I wept as I wrapped my arms around her. She was as rigid as a board, but I was already committed to the warm gesture.

"This time she lied," she continued. "She told me that if I would get rid of it, that she would take me back, and here I am with you."

I tried not to take offence at her remark. After all, I was the one who broke the dam, so what if I got a little wet? We continued the conversation over breakfast in bed. I ended up staying in her room, talking about her plans, dreams and disappointments. She said that she deeply regretted not having the second baby. She said she wished she could have given the baby to me. We hugged and cried.

Things were different between us after that. Oh, she still sneaked out a few times and lied to us, but it was evident it was getting more and more difficult to do. Once, when caught in a lie, she told us that it hurt to lie to us, because we loved her anyways. I had to smile.

After a six-month stay, Caitlyn was returned to her mother. At the end of the hearing, she turned into a cold stranger. Hugs and good-byes were quick and to the point. I had expected tears, but then realized that she simply had to cut us off. Perhaps we did make a difference.

We were sure of this one thing, we did not want to deal with any more teenagers. They were definitely in a class of their own. Since our younger children had not yet crossed that threshold, we would stick with the familiar and only take young ones. Okay...eventually we would only take young ones.

"Hello?" I answered the phone. "She's seventeen? Okay, bring her. We'll see you around six o'clock."

What was I thinking?

Becky

What a sweet girl. I was enthralled by her charm, but because of recent past experience, I questioned her sincerity. Becky had, in fact, called the county office herself, and asked to be placed in foster care until she could obtain a lawyer and be granted emancipation. It was ten months before her eighteenth birthday, and she had refused to stay in the same house with her father. She had recently learned through the local newspaper that her dad was being charged with assaulting a minor. The alleged victim was her best friend. This apparently happened right under her nose. She was greatly appalled and embarrassed by her family and wanted nothing more than to be free of them.

Becky remained with us for only two weeks, but she was a true joy to be around. She planned to transfer to a different high school, graduate and attend college. While waiting for her emancipation to be finalized, Becky agreed to move in with an older cousin, which was an approved placement for her. I hated to see her go, but I understood why.

I bumped into her cousin later that year. She was disappointed by the fact that Becky had been granted her freedom and had decided to marry her high school sweetheart without finishing school. Her cousin felt this was her plan the entire time, and that it had little to do with finishing school or attending college.

Becky was very mature for her age and made her own decisions. I believe she was genuinely disgusted with her father's behavior and later conviction. Once emancipated, her decisions were hers to make.

A few years down the road, we received a Christmas card from Becky and her new family. She had obtained her GED and had given birth to two beautiful babies. She was happy to express her gratitude for being able to share her life with us for a brief time. I smiled as I hung the card alongside the many other card we had received from friends and family that year.

Sometimes we would hear from a mutual friend of ours that she and her family were doing well. After we moved from that county, we eventually lost contact with her. The time we spent with Becky was a short chapter in our lives, but a very sweet one. One we will forever cherish.

Kissy Fur and Terri

I was dressed for a special service we were to attend one Sunday evening. As soon as our babysitter arrived, we started for the door before pausing briefly to answer the telephone. Jake smiled as he scribbled down information. I recognized the look on his face; I had seen it before. I could tell, from his side of the conversation, that we were about to retrieve a bundle, and it sounded like a small bundle at that.

"Is it a boy or girl?" I blurted out.

He laughed, hung up the receiver, and answered, "Both."

Change of plans. We asked the sitter to please stay until we returned from the local police station. We drove the half mile down the hill to the station, and struggled to keep ourselves from running anxiously into the building. We felt like eager children on Christmas morning. We could not keep our hearts from racing in. There on the front desk, an angelic little girl with big blue eyes and curly blonde hair, greeted us with outstretched arms. Jake instantly picked her up. She clung to his neck as if she knew him. I sighed in awe and sadness at her response.

Suddenly, I spied two little bare feet kicking out from under a baby blanket on the other desk. I quickly gathered the squirming infant into my arms. He smelled funny and was sticky from head to toe. His hair was light brown, and his eyes were a magical, crystal blue. He was clothed in a droopy diaper and a filthy blue t-shirt. It was a cold, March evening. He was obviously not dressed for the weather. His thin baby blanket was the only shelter from the cold outdoors. It would simply have to do until we got them home.

The kind-hearted police officer handed us a legal form to sign as we snuggly held our prized bundles. The infant boy was just six months old. The girl seemed to be around two years of age; we were not quite sure, and their names were as yet unknown. For the next three days, we simple referred to them as, "Baby Girl" and "Baby Boy." It was not very creative, but it would suffice.

We later learned their names and the circumstances around the placement. I nicknamed the boy, Kissy Fur. It appeared that their mom and dad had been in a violent argument and had walked out of their apartment, leaving the babies alone. Their father was charged with child endangerment, since he had been the last to leave. The mother was not charged, but both were required to attend anger management class, as well as parenting classes, before the children would be returned to them. This was meant to be a temporary placement that ended up lasting for three-and-a-half years. Housing became the mother's new problem, and it seemed that one thing after another kept the children from returning home.

We fell in love with the little cherubs. Terri was such a delight. We discovered she was only eighteen-months-old, instead of two years. She was very protective of her little brother. He was such a cute baby. Terri watched me intently during feedings or a diaper change, as if I were doing it all wrong. Once, I was preparing to change the baby's diaper, the phone rang. When I returned from a short conversation, I found that she had already changed the baby. No kidding, she did a great job. I could tell she had done it before.

We had some concerns about six-month-old Kissy Fur. He did not act like an average infant his age. He was rather docile. He was easily frightened and did not like to be cuddled. He had rigidness in his body that didn't seem quite right. He stiffened when he was picked up, yet he became floppy when placed in a high chair or bouncy seat. He did not have any physical problems, but he was highly agitated at times.

After a few months of encouragement through play and touch, along with gentle cuddling, Kissy Fur's "lights" came on. He began to smile and giggle when he was being held. He was beginning to catch up with other babies his age, right where he needed to be.

Four months into the placement, he was then ten months old. He slid out of the highchair and hit his head above the nose and eyebrow. He was taken to the hospital where he had x-rays and ten stitches. Soon after, he began having screaming fits. As he grew, they became more intense. These were not regular temper tantrums, but seemed more like uncontrollable outbursts. One of his typical fits would start with a cry that would quickly escalate into a kicking, screaming, and head-banging adventure. We tried talking to him. We tried to kiss it away. We even began to resort to bribery, promising to give him something special, anything, if he would just try to settle down. Nothing worked.

The spells occurred up to three times a day. They came without warning, sometimes lasting for more than an hour at a time. As soon as he began an episode, I would remove anything that might endanger him. I would then find a comfortable position to hold him until it passed. As he thrashed, I would sing softly into his ear, and gently rock him until his cry eased up and his once rigid body became limp. I would continue to talk to him as he seemed to return to life, uninterrupted. He would be left totally exhausted, and drift off to sleep. I was left worn-out, with bumps and bruises on my head, neck or chest. When he was old enough to talk, he would say, "Sorry Mommy, I love you."

"I love you too, baby." I would reply, ever so drained.

The spells continued day after day, week after week, month after month. After a long while of being told by his pediatrician, that he was just having temper tantrums, we were able to convince him to perform some tests. We needed answers. Maybe he was having seizures. Maybe he had some food allergies. There were so many questions.

The CAT scan showed negative for any signs of seizure activity. What? We were told, once again that Kissy was a temperamental child and, since the cause was not evident, we were left to deal with it for years. And deal, we did. To be quite honest, there were more times than I care to share, that I wanted to "throw in the towel," and give up. Maybe a different foster home could deal better with this than we could. There was no way on earth we could give up on him. That would have benefitted no one. With the love and support of my husband, who took over the meals or laundry, whatever needed to be done, while Kissy and I were "dealing," we were compelled to keep going. We pushed forward, sometimes rather drudgingly, but forward nonetheless.

The children became a big part of our lives. They were welcomed by our family and church. It was amazing to watch them grow and play. They were happy children; however, the court ordered bi-weekly visits with their biological mother, left both of them emotionally stressed out as well as physically ill. They had trouble eating meals after visits, and unfortunately, when they did eat, they would both vomit.

Kissy's screaming fits soon increased to nights, as well as in the daytime. Sometimes two to three times a night. Both children received counseling, though I'm not sure how much it helped. We soon grew tired of the sleepless nights that were now part of the "norm". We were powerless when we sought help. His counselor acted as if we were making the whole thing up. We decided to just deal with it and keep him safe. We would explain his odd behaviors when he acted up in public. Since it was unpredictable, we had to be flexible and prepared at all times.

One day, when we were in in a restaurant, Kissy became enraged because his fries were too big. They were steak fries, not the kind you would get at a fast food place. The minute he began to cry, I took him to the ladies room, sat on the toilet seat and held him close as he wailed. He screamed for forty-five minutes, non-stop. I gently rocked him and kissed his head. At some point, an older woman used the restroom beside me, washed her hands, and then firmly planted her chubby feed in front of my stall.

"What in the world did you do, beat him?" she asked rather snootily.

I was irritated and completely drained. I pushed the stall door open with my foot, looked her square in the eye and asked,

"Ma'am, would you like to try holding him for a while?"

"Well I never!" she blasted, storming out of the restroom.

"I guess not then," I quipped.

I was too pooped to put up with her remark. I did not feel I owed her any explanation. I was shocked by her outspokenness, so I joined her snub club, momentarily. There was simply too much up with which to put!

As soon as Kissy was settled down, I washed his face and mine. We returned to the table where the rest of the family was finishing their dessert. The kind, understanding waitress brought him and I a fresh plate of food. He was more than happy to eat his giant fries, and life went on.

When the visits turned from bi-weekly to bi-weekly, overnight weekends, both children had more than difficult times. Every other Friday, we took the twosome and a small suitcase to their mother's apartment, where they would both scream and cry and struggle to stay in the car. Once outside the car, Kissy would scream and wrap himself around Jake's legs so tightly, that he would have to pry him from his legs. It was a nasty scene that drew plenty of unwanted attention from the neighbors. It was heart-wrenching.

This horrific scene played out over the next six months. The children were then returned to their mother. This ripped our hearts into shreds. They had been in our home for three-and-a-half years. At the time, there were no time limits for parents to get their act together. We had seen and heard of children who were in foster care for their entire childhood, without hope of either returning home, or being placed for adoption. They were in limbo, neither living here nor there. This we found, was a sad fact of life. But, we thought, at least we were able to help them for a while.

After the children were returned to their home, we were told to "move on," and to not make any contact with them. We lived in the same town, so we decided to wait and see what would happen. We are so glad we did. We were contacted by their mother a few days later. She expressed that the children really missed us and wanted to spend the weekend with us. We threw caution to the wind and were glad to have them visit with us as long as they wanted. This soon became a weekly trend. We were not financially compensated for our time, but we enjoyed every minute we had to spend with them. We were still "Mom and Dad."

The weekly visits continued until my husband and I were appointed to pastor a church that was located over a hundred miles away. Because of the distance, we were only able to have visits over holiday weekends. Over the next five years, the visits were enjoyed extensively over the summers as well.

In that time, Kissy's behaviors became less frequent, but were incredibly more intense. He began kicking and hitting his mother, during his "episodes". He started swearing and running out the door, slamming it behind him. He returned home when he felt like it. His mother decided to send him to a juvenile detention center. He was ten years old. We were not at all happy with his mothers' decision, but we had no idea what we could do about it.

Since it was a juvenile hearing that required the presence of the county office, we decided to take a risk and show up at the hearing. I cannot tell you who informed us that there even was a hearing. She could have lost her job. It seemed a few people cared about Kissy as much as we did. We showed up at the hearing and declared that we were willing to take him back as a non-relative placement, since we already had a history with him. We would not have any monetary compensation, but we did not care at this point. We stressed that we believed he did not belong in a detention center.

His mother was, at first, angry that we had appeared in court, but she agreed with the recommendation to place her son with us for further care. One of the stipulations given by the court was, that he would attend intensive counseling services with possibly being placed on medications to help his mood. His state-funded insurance would cover any medical or psychiatric conditions.

We were happy to once again have Kissy living in our home. With a newly changed law in place, he would be released for adoption after fifteen months in placement with us. After some months of counseling, a diagnosis of Oppositional Defiance Disorder, and possible Bipolar Disorder, was made. He was prescribed mood-enhancing medications. Coincidently, it was an anti-seizure medicine commonly prescribed for seizure disorder. Since it seemed to work for the most part, I often wonder if he had indeed been having seizures all the years before. He still had some explosive episodes, but they were limited to approximately one a month. He was never aggressive towards us, nor did he swear. It was a long, hard journey that was well worth the trouble. When he went through the typical teen-age years, with other outrageous outbursts, I often thought, "I'm doing this, why?"

After two years, the county office called to see if we would be willing to intervene for Terri, who was becoming truant in seventh grade. She used to love school and was a pretty good student. Something was going on as she began skipping and missing more and more school. I felt her truancy was nothing more than a desperate cry for help. With her mother's "revolving door" of boyfriends, I feared for the worst. When our fears became a reality, Terri came to live with us, and her journey of healing began.

Eighteen months later, the children were adopted into our family forever. They continued a relationship with their mother and visited her, on their terms, when we were in the neighborhood. My husband, Jake, performed funeral services for their grandmother, when she passed away. This was not as awkward as you would think, since their biological family was all very supportive of us raising the children. Earlier, when they were small, Jake also involved, as a minister, with the family when their twenty-four-year-old aunt died of Leukemia. We had counseled with the family, and we were there when they made the decision to discontinue life support, as she slipped into a deep, irreversible coma. He not only performed her funeral, but gained respect and support from the family.

The years that followed were much more than comfortable. Terri and Kissy's mother became more open to their lives away from her. They pursued a grown-up relationship with her as well as their father, who has since passed away. Of course, Jake preached at his funeral.

It has been a long road for both children, who are now adults. Kissy seemingly grew out of his spells and discontinued his medications. He has a full-time job and a steady girlfriend. He does wonderful remodeling work and has grown into a nice young man.

Terri lives alone with her three children and is an awesome hair dresser. She is quite a young lady and a friend to have. She is especially close to her adoptive sisters and maintains a relationship with her mom. She has had to battle her own demons and we expect a full recovery. Through all of their ups and downs, I guess you can say it's a happy ending...at least where it comes to love and a sense of belonging.

Three Little Princesses

A set of bunk beds and a small toddler bed were quickly filled after one phone call. Three little blue-eyed, blonde princesses were promptly delivered to our front door. Meagan, the oldest, was a tall, thin six-year-old in first grade. Haley, who was just about to turn five, had beautiful, wispy, blonde curls. Her eyes were piercing, crystal blue. Tiny, dimple-faced Sara was eighteen months old. Her silky brown hair ended at shoulder length. The pink barrette holding her bangs in place, kept sliding down and needed frequent adjustments.

The girls came to our home to recover from multiple abuses. Wounds inflicted by their own biological father ran deep. Allegedly, he had attempted to harm the oldest, and when she refused to cooperate, he turned to the two younger sisters, leaving them with scars that ran deeper than flesh. It was evident that their little wings were tattered, torn and bloodstained.

It was an arrogant thought, on my part, to think that I could take them in my arms and simply kiss the pain away. I would have thought I would have known better. I bore my own secret scars of childhood. They were buried deep. I tried not to think about it. I could not, however, grasp the enormity of their pain that was inflicted by their dad. They were frightened and confused. Someone needed to pay for this heinous crime, and the overwhelming evidence the girls carried. I hated what this man had done to his children.

Meagan, the oldest, believed that she was being punished for tattling on her dad. She knew he was going to jail, and she understood why. She carried extreme, unearned guilt for the pain her sisters endured, and she had somehow avoided.

The girls were enrolled in intensive psychological therapy to aid in their hopeful recovery. Meagan's guilt let do depression and thoughts of suicide. It was terrifying to think that a six-year-old would ever consider taking her own life. She had, at one time, threatened to lie down on the road in front of our house, and let a truck run over her. We lived on a busy street used by coal trucks and petroleum carriers. I immediately contacted Meagan's caseworker and psychologist, who instantly placed her on suicide alert. Our home was dead-bolted, and I did not leave her side until the crisis passed. It was weeks before she seemed relaxed and safe.

Meagan, the main caregiver, decided to focus on her sister's recovery. At age six, she was loving and nurturing to the younger ones. I believe this helped her as well as the two little sisters. It was apparent to me, that they were used to her loving care. I gave her space to help them in any way she wanted. I could not tell her that I was in charge. I think she needed the outlet.

Haley, the middle child, was angry and impulsive. She always answered sharply, even when simply asked what she would like to eat or what she wanted to play with. She was a thumb-sucker. Her front teeth stuck out a lot, which gave her tiny face and impish look, like an elf. She was small for her age, but she carried a mountain of fury. Her favorite expression were too explicit for this writer to type. On several occasions, I had to remove her from a public place while covering her obscenities with my hand. More than once, I had to escort her from church when she would go into a rage and utter things that made sailors sound like Sunday school teachers. Oh what colorful metaphors that spewed from her darling, pursed lips!

Haley also love to use her common, one-finger sign language skills to get her point across. One evening, during vacation bible school, she decided to let one of the older women know exactly what she thought of her. I could only guess what happened when I noticed the greatly put-out woman charging across the parking lot to get my attention.

"Uh oh," I whispered as the woman's niece cut her off to give me the heads up. I took Haley's hand and asked her calmly to apologize to the old woman. She arrived at an alarming pace.

Haley looked up and said, "I'm sorry."

"WELL I NEVER!" snipped the angry senior.

I quickly explained a few details of the girl's rough lives, without breaking confidences.

"Well, God bless her little heart," She quietly replied. After that, they left each other alone, to my pleasure.

Sara was a beautiful baby. She had a lazy eye that appeared to be crossed at times. She seemed like a normal toddler. She was cuddly and loved to be held. She was a calm, loving child. She was relaxed and responded appropriately to affection. However, she had some self-mutilating behaviors. She had an old cigarette burn on her arm that she constantly picked at, reopening the wound. She also had a small scratch on her nose that turned into a bigger gash, by her constant digging. I tried to keep her fingernails short, but she seemed to keep picking until she drew fresh blood.

Children's Services called to inform me that I needed to take the two younger girls to a certain doctor, in a neighboring town. He would be taking photos of the girls to be used at their father's upcoming trial. This was going to be an explicit exam and photo session. I was told to prepare the girls emotionally for the exam and to remain with each girl as the pictures were taken. How was I to prepare them for this? How could I prepare myself? I invited my mom to go with me for support.

After signing the girls in at the front desk, I took them to the dressing room where they changed into teddy bear covered gowns. Wearing nothing but the gowns, the girls played innocently in the waiting area, giggling as they shared toys and books with each other. My stomach hurt with anticipation. I did not want to be there.

Haley was called into the exam room first. She bounced into the room and jumped onto the table as the dr. instructed. She smiled and rolled over onto her belly as the nurse requested. I was instructed to move toward Haley and entertain her during the intrusive, uncomfortable exam. I was sickened as I overheard the doctor dictate his findings to the nurse. Leaning in toward Haley, I whispered into her ear. I told her that she was a beautiful princess and that she was going to be okay. My voice was soft and calming. On the inside, my heart cried out.

"How could anyone hurt a little girl in this way?" I screamed silently. "What gave him the right to violate her and rob her of her childish innocence? This type of violence should never be perpetrated on anyone, much less a child, and by her own father! I hope he pays for this. He just sentenced this baby to life in this prison! Oh, please God, help her through this. Help me to help her."

"Okay, we are finished," the doctor interrupted my thoughts.

I gathered Haley in my arms and carried her back to the dressing room, kissing her little head.

"Will my daddy go to jail now?" she asked, fully understanding the reason for such an exam. Her words caught me off guard.

"I sure hope so, baby," I answered, choking back a tear. "I sure hope so."

I handed Haley to my mom, who was playing with the baby. I could only imaging the tattered look on my face, by the way my mom looked at me. I felt near to crying out, but the task had not ended. It was now little Sara's turn. She smiled as she toddled to the examining room. I really did not want to be a part of this. I know it was important to document the damages, but I had already seen the scar. I did not want to know more.

Sara was not toilet trained as of yet. Every time her diaper was changed, the evidence of the crime against her stared at me. There was little question to the cause of such damage. It was a constant reminder of the absolute torture this child must have endured. There were times I could not bring myself to change her. This is when my teen daughters would step in and help me.

As I lay Sara on the examination table, and as the nurse prepared her for the camera, the camera bulb popped abruptly, startling us all. The doctor did a quick exam and stated that he had seen enough, and the report would be completed within a week. As he thanked me for bringing the girls, he wiped a tear from his cheek, and left the exam room. The nurse followed him out the door without a word. I gathered Sara into my arms and took her to the other room to dress her.

I sat silently in the front seat as my mom drove us home. I had nothing to say. My mind was in a whirlwind. What I was thinking was too vile to share with anyone. I wanted to take a shower and wash the horror down the drain. I could not share my feelings with my mom. She had no idea what I had gone through as a child, and how I was being forced to relive the trauma. The little princesses in the back seat seemed untouched by the events of the last hour. I was screaming and crying on the inside, I wanted to vomit.

Once in the shower, I sobbed, unsuccessfully trying to scrub away the day. I felt as though I had defiled the girls. I detested the role I had played in the exam room, even though I know it had to be done. I knew I needed to be there to comfort them. As the steaming water poured over my head, the memories of my own childhood events flooded my mind. I knew that in order to help the girls; I would need to seek counsel for myself.

Healing was slow and certain. The girls and I attended weekly sessions at a mental health facility. It was a process that would take time and patience for everyone. I knew they would require long-term therapy. I was in a Christian counselling program myself, separate from them. I was willing to do what I could to help them in their recovery. I figured anything we did would help us all. We talked a lot about inappropriate behaviors and bad language. We discussed the differences between appropriate and inappropriate touching. I tried to help them understand how grownups were to act around children. They were easy to redirect and had very little difficulty expressing themselves. Sometimes we laughed together and sometimes we cried.

I admit to being overprotective of the girls. When they were eventually sent home to live with their mother and her boyfriend, I was more than outraged. Deep down inside, I had hoped the girls would not have been sent home. It started with overnight weekend visits at first, then they went home for good. It was a slow tearing of my heart, but I knew the girls were delighted to go home.

As we packed their belongings, I asked them if they would like to take their bed sheets and blankets home with them. They responded enthusiastically to the notion. I was more than happy to give them the character set. Besides, I didn't think I could bear to look at their empty beds as it was. It had proven to be therapeutic for me to change the bedding with each new placement. It offered closure and anticipation for the next children who would use the empty beds.

Along with the departure of children came unanswered questions that plagued me. I wondered how the little princesses were doing, now that they were home with their mother. I discovered that sometimes it is best to never have these questions answered at all. I decided that with the girls, I would not even ask. I was informed, however.

The girls lived twenty miles away from us and we did not see each other for years. However, one summer they showed up at our church camp. Apparently, the girls attended a street ministry within walking distance of their home, and were eventually invited to our camping program. I was not prepared to see them, but there they were.

It was exciting to see them, and only the two older girls had remembered me. Meagan and Haley seemed well and happy. Sara did not know me, and we chose not to give her all of the information. She was dressed in mismatched clothes that were too tight, and were visibly uncomfortable for her. Her worn out sandals were too small. Her hair was dirty and unkempt. Sara seemed to be lost. She also seemed to be heavily sedated. She roamed around, not connecting with the other children or adults. She did not answer when spoken to. She hissed and growled when approached by other children. Although several staff members tried to interact with her, she ignored them and walked away. During class, she simply closed her eyes. She seemed to be hiding from the world around her.

Medication had been given to the camp nurse for Sara. She was instructed on administering Sara's medication, but expressed concern at the medicines effect on her. Even though the correct amount was given, Sara seemed incredibly drowsy. It was difficult to determine how much of her behavior was deliberate and how much was drug induced. The nurse contacted her mother and she confirmed that the medication dosage was correct. Sara had apparently been violent in the past and had been prescribed a strong sedative to help control the outbursts. I was heartbroken to see how much she had digressed over the last few years. At eight years old, she seemed to be less than a shell of a girl who once had been a cuddly, affectionate toddler. I did not want to know what else had happened to her that caused this deterioration. My heart would not allow me to go any further.

I learned that later that summer, the girls' father had been released from jail after serving a mere seven-year sentence for his crime. Seven years! To me, it seemed that at least one of these little girls received a life sentence.

Jerry

Of all the angels that have entered our home I believe Jerry was the most real. He was six years old and did not walk. There was nothing wrong with his legs; he simply preferred to get around by crawling and walking upright upon his knees. His mother had serious mental health issues of her own, and when his mother was no longer able to take care of him, he was placed in foster care.

Jerry was born with multiple diagnosis. He had beautiful, droopy brown eyes and quite a catching laugh. His hair was short and dark brown. He had already lost his baby teeth, and had a brand-new set of permanent teeth in the front, primed and ready to go. He constantly grinded his teeth. It made a sound that could set your nerves on end. Jerry chewed on anything that could not get out of his way, including people! He even chewed on his own fingers, which accounts for the missing piece of his "pinky" finger. His teeth looked like a horse's teeth, and trust me, it did not affect his bite. Not only did we need to protect ourselves from him, but he had to be protected from himself.

We first met Jerry in the emergency room, where he was receiving treatment for a number of severe bites on his forearms. They were not only self-inflicted, they were infected and oozing. He was wrapped to the elbows in gauze and surgical tape. Before the nurse could warn me, he took a small taste of my left

31

arm. I did not think I tasted so well, but he giggled hilariously. It was as if he waited all day to do that.

His bandaged arm made him look as though he had been in a terrible accident. The dressing would need to be changed twice a day. Once we were home with this angel, we needed a plan. In order to keep Jerry's bandages on after cleaning, I would wrap one arm at a time in the gauze. I then place an adult-sized tube sock on each arm, pull them up to his shoulders, and pin them in place with large diaper pins. This gently covered the wounds and made it more difficult for him to tear off the bandages and cause more damage. Many times between changes, he would chew and suck on the socks, soaking them through to the gauze. The socks would then have to be thrown away with the gauze. It was a daily challenge to keep him Jerry safe.

Jerry was quite a contortionist. He was as flexible as a rag doll. He had to sit in a highchair with the straps fastened to keep him from slithering, like warm gelatin to the floor. He could not use neither utensils, nor dishes. It was soon determined, that anything that entered his mouth was not coming out again. Finger foods, pardon the pun, were a must for him. We soon learn to cut food into small, bite-size pieces and quickly toss the food onto his highchair tray to escape injury. He had the table manners of Helen Keller.

Jerry love to eat pizza. One time, on an outing with our family at the local Pizza shop, Jerry became excited about his food and lost his patience. He began to snort and laugh hysterically when the waitress brought our pizza. I cut it up, and blew on it to cool it down, all the while Jerry was hitting all the high notes. As I carefully tossed Jerry's slice onto his highchair tray, it was a noisy explosion of absolute victory! I have never witnessed the disappearance of pizza at the speed of light, and this after raising teenagers! We were surprised and amused at his actions. However, the big, burly guy seated directly behind Jerry was obviously put out by his behavior.

"People ought to make their kids behave in public!" He snapped. We politely told him we were sorry to disturb him. He reeled around in his seat and continued to badmouth poor Jerry. We decided that in the future, we would ask for more private seating so as not to upset other guests.

Jerry was the epitome of innocence. He had no way of comprehending how his behaviors affected others, and there was no real meaningful interaction with our dear, little angel. Jerry had also been diagnosed with autism, which further impaired his learning and communication skills. He needed constant supervision and was, in actual fact, much like an infant. He wore diapers. He could not drink from a cup. He still chewed toys much as a toddler. For his safety and our peace of mind, Jerry slept in a crib.

One time, during his evening bath, Jerry had a bowel movement in the bathtub. Before I could stop him, he had scooped up his fecal matter and shoved it all in his mouth it while I was looking for something to fish it out with. My teenage son, and his friend ran into the bathroom to see why I was screaming. With one look at the scene unfolding, they gagged and ran out the front door. I put a large amount of toothpaste on a washcloth and proceeded to clean out Gary's mouth, praying that I would finish with as many fingers as I had started out with. Talk about a dirty mouth! This was the nastiest one I had ever encountered. I found pleasure in the fact that my son and his friend had been trying to gross me out for some time. Mysteriously though, after this incident, they stopped trying.

We made bibs out of towels to keep Jerry dry, and to give him something harmless to chew on. After his arms were healed up, I ordered a pair of small, adult sized arm braces to wear on him at night to keep him from chewing on his hands or arms. They were made of soft leather, strong enough that Jerry could not chew through them. As time went on, and Jerry seemed to have calmed down, he was able to go throughout the day without any coverings on him at all. He was able to play without harming himself. He still chewed on some things, but his chewing was more controlled. He seemed so happy and contented in his little world. He was a handful, to say the least. How we enjoyed having him visit until his wounded wings were healed.

Jerry went back home with his mother after six months. His home life followed the same pattern though, and after two years, he returned once again to our home to recover from the damages. This time, he was walking on his own and able to reach many things, as we soon learned. His hands were again torn and tattered, but not as severe as they had been in the past.

Jerry stayed a month or two the second time. Shortly after returning to his home, we were approached about providing long term placement and possible adoption. It was getting to be too difficult for his mother to care for him, along with her own problems. My heart told me to take him back and adopt him, but my head spoke wisdom. I knew I was not going to be able to handle his ever-increasing physical needs. I have chronic problems with my back and could not continue with the lifting and handling of this now eight-year-old boy. Therefore, Jerry was placed with the family who had cared for him once before, and was able to devote more time and much needed attention to. It was a decision that I wished I did not need to make.

Jerry is now in his 20s. He is the same age as one of our adopted sons. I pray he is healthy. I say this because I learned that during his stay with us, he was in remission from leukemia. One fact that remains, is that Jerry is truly an angel. He touched our lives and filled with joy for having known him for a moment in time.

Kyle and Aries

They were cute as they could be. They were a beautiful, African-American brother and sister tag team. Aries was a four-year-old girl who obviously the boss. Kyle, her little brother, was two. Their older siblings were placed in other foster homes. I think I got the pick of the litter. They were absolutely adorable. It was a challenge for me, to clean and maintain their coarse hair. I managed to learn how to keep it moist, and even learned how to braid it and put small beads in the tiny strands of three.

As little boys are, Kyle was fascinated with our sandbox. He would play in it for hours. It became a bigger job to keep his hair nice, though. No matter how clean, or how beautiful the children looked at their visits with their mother, she would let me know that I did not know how to take care of her children. I knew that. I learned to ignore his mother's snide remarks at each visit concerning their hair.

Aries was quite bossy. She must have been accustomed to telling the other children what to do, what to eat, and what to say. Kyle seem to look to her for all the answers. One day as we were eating dinner, I offered Kyle a spoonful of peas. He looked at his sister and asked, "Aries, does I like little green bean balls?"

"Yes." He proceeded to eat his peas.

Kyle and Aries made us laugh often. They were friendly and apt to say anything. One day, Aries said, "My mom is really funny like you, when she sniffs baby powder up her nose." We knew her mom had a drug problem, but did not realize she did it in front of the children. That was one of those red flag opens. I immediately made the caseworker aware of this information.

It was a joy to have them around. They were lovable and just plain adorable. We took them camping, swimming, and to the amusement park. They were in our home in sickness and in health. Once, they both had a severe case of chickenpox. We were more in for more than our share of fun. Yeah, right.

Oatmeal baths, trimmed fingernails, and allergy medicine works fine, until we found out the hard way that Kyle was allergic to it. He had been given the required dosage, as had his sister. However, he decided one day to climb up into the cabinet after a dose and finish off the bottle. Fortunately, there was only about a teaspoon left in the bottle. Unfortunately, it was enough to send him over the edge.

After his sister told on him for drinking the rest of the medicine, I noticed that he was acting peculiar. I first noticed him standing, leaning on our water cooler with one leg drawn up, like a flamingo. He tilted his little head looked at me and said,

"Hello, Annie." in his deep voice.

I asked him if he was feeling okay.

He simply answered, "I don't know, does I feel okay, Aries?"

She wasn't sure, so I kept an eye on him as he played. He continued to stand like a flamingo and seemed dazed and confused. He even stopped asked in his sister's opinion. I called his caseworker to let her know what was going on and to see if he had any allergies. She informed me that she would contact his biological mother and then get back to me. I also called the phone number on the medicine bottle, describing his symptoms, to see if he had possibly overdosed. I felt like a total shmuck.

The person on the other end of the phone told me to keep an eye on Kyle, and to call back in two hours to give an update on his condition. After an hour, I became more and more concerned about him. When I called the company again, I was told to take him to the hospital immediately. I called for the ambulance. As he was being assessed, Kyle's caseworker called to inform me that Kyle was severely allergic to the medication I had given him. On top of that, he had a heart murmur. She told me I should call an ambulance. I told her we were already in the ambulance, and on our way to the hospital.

Once in the emergency room, the on-call Dr. prescribed time. Time for the medication to work its way through Kyle's system. Over the next seven hours, I sat in a chair and watched him hallucinate, talking nonstop in his deep, little voice. The Dr. reassured me that it would pass, and there would be no long-term effects. Still, it was very difficult to watch. I then contacted my husband, who was on his way back from out of town, and asked him to stop by the hospital on his way home. I needed him to stop and pick us up, since I has ridden to the hospital in the ambulance with Kyle. I hoped that we would be ready to go home by the time he arrived.

After five hours of continual nonsense, I laid my head at the foot of Kyle's bed and began to laugh hysterically. I laughed until I cried. Kyle told me that there were a cars under the bed, and I needed to be careful that I did not get run over. There were also horses on the ceiling. A nurse passing by, stopped in to see if I was okay. Kyle then asked the nurse for a bug sandwich. We both laughed, and she brought us a small snack in hopes that he would try to eat something. I was famished. Could I get a cracker?

Kyle could not drink from a straw, when given orange juice. He laughed as he watched me show him how. He took a bath with a banana, smashing it all over his chest. He then rubbed a graham cracker on his hair, sending it crumbling down his head. He looked up at me and said,

"It must be raining or something."

He did not know where he was who he was or who I was for that matter. He didn't really care. The hours seemed eternal.

The doctor stopped by once more, assuring me that it would soon be over. He told me to alert the staff when I noticed any change. Two hours later, my husband entered the emergency room. When Kyle saw him, he said, "Hi Jake, where's Aries?"

He had returned to us. I called for the Dr. After a quick examination, Kyle was released from the hospital. We were told that we could take him home as soon as he had something to eat. By then he knew what to do with the food, and seemed to be a bit curious as to why we were all looking at him. What a day!

That night was sleepless. I put his little bed in our bedroom so I could keep him from roaming through the house while we slept. Several times, I was awakened by the light. Kyle would repeatedly turn it on and take clothes out of a basket, and put them on the bed. He would then put the clothes back in the basket. The next day, around six am, he fell asleep. He and I then slept until dinnertime.

I admit that I was feeling a bit incompetent over the whole matter, but I learned to start asking questions when children were placed with us, like perhaps, do they have any allergies?

Hanna and Bo

Another brother and sister team came to our home to stay. Bo, the three-year-old boy, was a very pleasant little guy, who much like the last little boy, was highly dependent on his older sister. Hannah, at six years old, had been the leader of the pack of five younger siblings. Things at home had gone from bad to worse, when their mother was sent to prison for credit card fraud. There was no one to care for the children. The children's father was in rehab.

Hanna seemed to have lived in a fantasy world. Most children love to watch children's movies starring their favorite characters. It is so wonderful for them to have an active imagination, but Hannah somehow crossed the line. She believed she was the star of the show. She would cry and argue if her belief was challenged. She declared she was a true princes and starred in all the cartoon films.

At first, we did not see any danger in her fantasy. Later, she was diagnosed with Personality Disorder and Attention Deficit Hyperactive Disorder. She had a difficult time separating truth from fantasy. It was very hard to believe her stories. We sought counsel and were instructed to try to help her keep her feet on the ground, so to speak. She was encouraged to play different roles, and to talk about being a regular, truthful little girl when not playing. She had a convincing way about her than it gotten her into trouble on several occasions.

Hannah was quite the drama queen. She had long, brown hair, big, brown eyes, and a Hollywood smile. She looked the part of an indian princes. She demanded center stage. She was adorable, but unpredictable. She screamed when she was upset or did not get her way. She had the high pitched, deafening type of squeal. It would cause a crowd to silence nearly in an instant.

One evening while playing outside in the spring, Hannah was running in the yard doing cart-wheels with the other children. She had shrieked enough for one evening. I gave her a final warning.

"One more scream, young lady, and you will get your bath, and go straight to bed!"

Fifteen minutes and a screech later, she was bathed and in bed, without a word. She simply did as she was told, without arguing, this time.

Early the next morning, I woke her up to get her ready for school. She got dressed, and I combed her hair. Suddenly, she handed me her shoe.

She said, "Annie, I can't put my shoe on." She continued, "It won't fit."

"What's wrong with your shoe?" I inquired.

"My foot is too fat!" Came the reply.

I immediately looked down at her foot. It was swollen twice the size of her other foot. "You are not going to school today, sweetheart. I'm taking you to the hospital to get your foot looked at." It was all I could think to say, without alarming her.

I could not believe that of all the times to scream or yell, she had said nothing about hurting her foot in the yard the night before. I felt bad, but what was I to do? On the way to the hospital, I told Hannah the story of "The Boy Who Cried Wolf. I explained that every time we tell a lie, it makes it harder to believe when we are telling the truth. I laughed as Hannah repeated the story to the receptionist in the emergency room. She shared the story with the radiology technician and eventually the Dr.

Thankfully, her ankle was not broken, but badly sprained. It was amazing to me that little bit of change in Hannah. After that grand adventure to the hospital, Hannah was not as much of the screamer she used to be. She was also beginning to be more truthful.

But Hannah had yet another side to her. She was a very promiscuous little girl. She sought inappropriate attention from teen boys, and men. She would try to wrap her arms around them after church, or try to crawl up on their lap when we were visiting. She was small for her age, and it first, it seemed cute. Then, I began to notice how uncomfortable our friends would become when she was around. It was like, they would quickly pat her on the head and then push her away. The final revelation though, was when she told me, quite frankly, that she knew how to "make a man happy."

"And how was that? I calmly asked.

"My mommy showed me how." She continued.

I was fairly alarmed. I explained appropriate touches as well as in appropriate touches. Unfortunately, she was quite fixated on the male anatomy, and after several attempts to make some friends, we decided she needed more one-on-one attention and some intense therapy to help her through her confusion.

We made the decision to have Hannah placed with a family who had a little girl the same age. Her counselor felt it was best for her to have a same age female with whom she could relate. The last I heard, her brother Bo was returned to his father and full biological siblings. Her half-brother was adopted by another family. Hanna was adopted by family with whom she was placed. At the time of this writing, Hannah is in her mid-twenties. I hope that she is doing well. I look at her photo sometimes, and see her beautiful Hollywood smile.

The Doll

At the park, one warm summer day, we noticed a little girl with long curly light brown hair. She had a beautiful olive complexion that enhanced her light green eyes. I thought she looked more than a little familiar. She had grown tall and thin. She was now seven years old. Her smile was bright and she pranced around the park, seemingly carefree. I was sure we knew her.

Adrienne had come to live with us when she was two years old. She stayed for nearly a year, before her young parents found appropriate housing. They were considered to be homeless and had been staying with various friends, which was not appropriate for the little girl. The grandmother had taken the child to help out, but children's services would not allow the grandmother to the loan to be alone with any child, due to her own mental health conditions. So, they decided to place her in foster care until their situation improved.

I really felt for the young mother, who was trying to regain custody of her daughter. The younger, immature father was still in high school. He seemed more interested in playing video games than in setting up housekeeping for his family. He did not work, and soon dropped out of school, and moved back home with his mother, who had previously denied that the child was even his. It seemed that it was up to the young mother, with the help of her own father, to get the family back together.

I would have to say that of all the children who had been placed in our home, this little girl had an affectionate, strong family bond. It was rare so far to see a supportive family unit who struggled to gather to make things better for the child. Even though it was mainly the mother and grandfather who were working toward reunification, they were persistent. This family always treated my husband and me with respect. During the six month review hearings, they were more than kind to us. They seem to understand that we were not the enemy, as other families sometimes believed. For once, it was a fairly comfortable relationship.

I enjoyed being able to provide a safe environment for such a little angel. She really was a pleasure. When Adrienne would visit her family, they were both kind and courteous to us. They often express their appreciation for all we were doing. It made us feel good about what we do, yet it is really uncommon to get a kind word from a biological parent, and probably for good reason. After all, I can't even imagine my responses to the ones who may have had my children in their care. I'm not here to pass judgment on the parents, but to provide loving care for children and families in need.

Adrienne was a fun loving child. Her favorite game was to sneak up on me and giggle, "I'm going to get you!" I would then sneak up on her. She had such an infectious laugh that made everyone want to play along. She loved to be dressed up with hair bows and lace. She loved dolls, shoes and purses. She was nurturing to teddy bears. She cuddled and kissed everything furry. She was absolutely an adorable, living, breathing baby doll.

When Adrienne was returned to her parents, who had found ample housing for her and the baby on the way, it was a bittersweet moment for us. Although we were not worried so much about her welfare, we were sad for her to go.

I collect porcelain dolls as a hobby. I received a beautiful surprise the Christmas after Adrienne left us. As I opened the box, tears rolled down my cheeks as I set my eyes on a beautiful doll. She had long, curly, brown hair. She had a beautiful, olive complexion that enhanced her light, green eyes. She had a beautiful, bright smile. My doll, suitably named Adrienne, sits quietly in an oak highchair in my dining room. When I look at her, I and tenderly reminded of a charming, little angel girl that passed through our lives, piercing our hearts.

From the Crack House to Our House

I believe the longest six months of my life were when TJ and Kayla stayed with us. They came from a middle-class family who were literally living in a crack house. Their parents hosted party after party, with all five of their children present. The children were totally unsupervised as the adults were high. According to the files, this was a constant occurrence, at least until they were raided by the police. They had tried to escape trial by leaving the state, but were extradited, along with the children, and returned to our state for the hearing. There was a possibility of jail time, but they lawyered up and opted for rehab. The children had to be split between three foster families.

We agreed to take the two youngest. From the moment they arrived, they were an absolute handful. All of our breakables were placed on upper shelves. Books and videos were also housed on high, to avoid eminent destruction. The three and four-year-old team were a circus act. They were constantly into something. They jumped on furniture, threw toys, and used coloring books and crayons as weapons. It was time for me to sharpen my parenting skills.

They unquestionably could not be left alone for the slightest moment. Table manners were nonexistent. TJ's favorite activity was to dismantle toys and furniture. He was quiet and cunning. We were stunned to learn how easily he could remove the bolts from the coffee table. It was totally unnoticed until the table mysteriously collapsed. He was compliant and happily led us to the bolts that were tactically lined up across the bookcase. He was proud of his work, however, he quickly learned how to screw the bolts back in place. He was scolded, and left the coffee table alone, for a little while. Once it was tightened by a ratchet, TJ was unable to budge the little bolts. And to think, just a few good twists of the wrist, mission impossible.

It was discovered, in chatting with other foster parents, that the other children were equally destructive in their new surroundings. None seemed to respond to redirection well. I was amazed to find out that all the responses were the same. They simply acted as if they did not know the rules. For instance, Kayla did not know she could not flush a doll down the toilet, or that hitting her brother in the head with a winter boot would make him cry. TJ did not know he was not allowed to spit juice across the table and his sister. Neither seemed to know that you were not supposed to pull the legs off a cat. (Full-grown cats seem resistant to any type of dismantling.) Who knew? The list of damages go on and on and on. I just choose to end this here.

TJ and Kayla were extremely dramatic. I found that this was probably a learned behavior. There was no doubt they learned from their mother. On one occasion, Kayla was running through the living room, jumping on the furniture, when she fell and hit her head on my fully assembled coffee table. She received a pretty good black eye from the incident, but I was grateful she did not need stitches. It was a beauty! She carried on for hours and insisted that one of the other children caused the accident. No one caused her to run and jump around like a nanny goat.

A few days later, the children were due for their weekly visit with their parents. I called the caseworker ahead of time to give her the "heads up" on Kayla's injury. Her mother had previously displayed outbursts in the office, and I wanted to prepare everyone for the visit, just in case. Shortly after our arrival, the caseworker took a look at Kayla's eye. She asked my husband and me to stick around after the visit so that they could take pictures to document the incident. No problem.

Two hours later, my husband, Jake and I returned to the office just in time to meet up with the parents and Kayla in the hallway. We walked into the office together. I just happened to notice Kayla's eye appeared to be worse than when we had first arrived. I asked her what happened. Her eye looked awful! Her mother acted nervous and quickly dismissed my question. When the caseworker began to take her by the hand to her cubicle, to take the pictures, I stopped her.

"Wait a minute," I interjected. "Let me see her."

"What's the problem?" Asked her mother.

"Hon," I motioned to Jake. "Go in the men's room and grab a wet paper towel."

"I need to leave now." The mother snipped. "Go ahead in, and take the pictures."

Jake quickly returned with wet paper towel. I then proceeded to wipe the entire "bruise" from her lower eye, and half from her eye lid, where the real bruising had occurred. This happened in plain view of office staff, and other foster parents, whose children were visiting their families. It was entertaining at best. Apparently, mom had some blue eye shadow and decided to enhance the photos, making Kayla's injury appear worse than it really was. I'm sure she thought this would be beneficial. When she realized her plan had failed, she became outraged and shouted,

"I don't know what's going on in your house, but it is evil!"

Without saying goodbye to her children, she quickly made a dramatic exit, slamming the door behind her. A united chuckle filled the room as I motioned for her caseworker to go ahead with the photo shoot. I found it hard to resist the temptation to open the door and quickly yell,

"Way to go cracker!" I did not.

Two weeks later, all five children were moved to adoptive home. Their mother and father relinquished their parental rights, and after finishing the required rehabilitation services, they promptly left the state and returned to the world that consumed them and shattered the family.

Crack Angel

We had been escorted to the housing projects, by the local police, to remove an angel. We were armed with a minivan and an infant seat. Yes, it was as if we were members of the local SWAT team. Our mission; to locate and snatch up, an infant boy, along this with as many disposable diapers and pieces of clothing that our arms could carry.

The kind officer who had given directions only moments ago now forced his way into the apartment at the objection of the female resident. We were careful to dodge the empty words of the girlfriend of the recently incarcerated mother of the said infant. She began to curse the attending officer. My heart was in my throat. He placed his hand on his side arm and asked,

"Would you also like to go to the station young lady?"

"No sir!" She answered nervously.

"Then step aside until we are finished here." The officer replied.

"Yes sir." Came her now humble reply.

She suddenly was more than happy to oblige the man in uniform. She offered me a bag for the baby bottles, and several cans of infant formula, I had just discovered on the kitchen table. She was obviously angry, but cooperative. It seemed we were doing something wrong. I wondered if what we were doing was even legal, after all, we had never actually gone to the homes of the soon-to-be foster children before, especially an extraction. But, since the police called us in on this one, we were obliged to help.

It was awkward in that we had just recently delivered Thanksgiving turkeys to needy families in the same apartment complex. I'm sure we were recognize by the crowd of spectators who had gathered outside. Things sure can get confusing. I could not believe we actually had been summoned to assist in the removal of a child from possible danger. It was exhilarating, but not so much as I would ever want to be in that particular position again. No thank you! Leave the "baby snatching" to the officials.

The baby was only one month old. His mother was addicted to crack cocaine and was high when she delivered her baby boy. Therefore, Joshua's tiny body was polluted by the drug, and he suffered the effects of drug withdrawal. He did not asked to be born into this mess, but he had to live out the daily torments. Joshua was very sensitive to noise. Any sudden clatter would send his tiny legs and arms flailing out of control. The only way to comfort him was to wrap him in a blanket and hold him snuggly. The ringing of the telephone set him off continually. When I would pick him up out of his little bassinet, he will cling to the sheets and pull the tiny mattress out. He slept most of the time, but was very easily awakened.

As time went on, Joshua gained a hearty appetite and was growing nicely. He smiled a lot, when he was not crying. His symptoms were lessening as time went on. It was too soon to tell whether he would have any long-term development issues. Children respond differently. I had no guidebook to show me the way. I hope that he would be okay and prayed that there would be no effect on him. Only time would tell.

After about a month, Joshua began sleeping through the night. His mother released from jail and did not attend the scheduled visits with her son. His mother later voluntarily signed for termination of her parental rights, placing Joshua up for adoption. It seems she was no longer interested in her child. I have to give her full credit for letting him go and giving him a second chance at life. Sadly, we have in the past, been witness to too many instances in which the child returned home to a worse situation than when he first left. This was one mother who thought the best interest of the child. She knew she could not care for him properly in her present state.

At four months old, Joshua was placed with an adoptive family. Because of our family circumstances at the time, we were unable to adopt him. Someone else though, was about to receive a tiny blessing. Not long after Joshua was transferred to his new home, I recognized his mother while out shopping. She seemed to be either drunk or high, and given her history, I was inclined to believe possibly both. She approached me and unflinchingly asked,

"How is Tyler?"

His name was actually Joshua, but she had already forgotten. I'm sure she knew the name of her drug supplier. I try not to judge, really, I do try.

Starving Angel

On my way to the hospital, I was flooded with questions racing through my mind. Ronnie was a small patient there. At 18 months old, he was severely malnourished and was diagnosed as a "failure to thrive" baby. He weighed a mere fifteen pounds on his admittance to the hospital, earlier that month. He did not like to eat it all. He had no verbal skills and was very frail, showing signs of malnutrition. His blond hair was thinning, and his belly was protruding. His big, brown eyes overshadowed his gaunt little face. He reminded me somewhat, of a sad little elf.

My assignment was to watch and learn how to feed and care for this petite, shadow of a boy. I wondered how difficult that would be. It was a challenge. Getting this food into his mouth was only half the battle. Getting him to actually swallow the food was a different story altogether. After visiting the baby in the hospital for five hours, we headed for home. I cried for quite a little while, thinking about this tiny, little body that was literally starving to death. I was not sure how successful I would be for my part of his recovery. He had been in the hospital for more than a month and had gained four pounds. I was praying for nothing short of a miracle.

Ronnie was released into our custody the following day. The doctor and his nutritionist stressed repeatedly, the importance of weekly height and weight measurements. If he lost as much as half an ounce, he would need to be returned to the hospital. It was determined that he was out of danger at the moment, but he needed to be monitored closely. The ride home was filled with even more questions. "What have I gotten myself into this time?" I asked myself a dozen times. I guess only time will tell.

Calorie! Calorie! Calorie! Everything that went into that baby's mouth was loaded with any extra calories I could find. Each and every meal counted, literally. Extra butter and heavy cream were added to mashed potatoes and scrambled eggs. Pudding or milkshakes were offered daily. After each of his high calorie meals, he was given a full, eight-ounce bottle of adult liquid calorie supplement. Fortunately, he loved the thick, sweet drink.

Each of Ronnie's five or six daily meals lasted roughly one hour. He could not be placed in a high chair and allowed to feed himself like other babies his age. He would not pick up a single morsel. Most of this food needed to be of smooth consistency. He would sit on my placemat on the table, facing me. Every meal was the same. I would put a spoonful of food in his mouth and place my forefinger across his lips. He would then clamped his mouth tightly and refuse to swallow the food. Tiny tears would trickle down his cheeks while I would speak, encouraging him to swallow the food. This would take at least an hour before he would finally give in and accept the food.

As soon as the first bite was down, I would then be able to give him two or three more mouthfuls before he clamped his jaws tight again. It was then that he would receive his liquid supplement to wash down what remained in his mouth. This dance was performed six to eight times a day, depending on how much food he consumed. I kept a record of meals and calories to ensure he was getting enough nutrition.

When we ate out, I usually retrieved Ronnie's meal as well as mine, from the buffet. This way, we could begin our ritual without disrupting the rest of the family. Those who were unaware of his situation looked on us with pity. Several times, I felt compelled to explain our particular table manners to the curious onlookers. Most had never heard of a baby with an eating disorder. Up until then, I had been one of them.

It was a hard job sometimes, but I believe myself to be quite stubborn. I had to be more willful the Ronnie, if we were to be successful at saving his life. I determined that this little boy would gain weight and grow. He did grow. After six months, his weight was up to twenty-six pounds! He was less lethargic after just a few months, and began moving around and playing with toys. He had a play therapist, who came to our home to work with him once a week. Before long, he began to talk. He called my daughter, "Gee-gee." He said, "Up, don't, bye-bye," and "no!"

Ronnie was a pleasant, little fellow who made no demands. His crib was located at the foot of our bed. In the morning, he love to crawl out of his crib and plop onto our bed. He would then race on hands and knees to the top of the bed to greet us. Many times we would smile quietly awaiting his little journey. It was wonderful to see this once sickly, quiet, shell of a boy transform into a lively toddler. I cannot assume all the credit for his recovery. I could only do so much. It was a God-given gift of patience that has seen many a child through a rough road.

Eventually, after Ronnie's second birthday, he was returned to his parents. My daughter collapsed into my arms as the caseworker took Ronnie to her car. She was so devastated by his departure that we decided not to take any children into our home, until she felt she was ready again. Clearly it was one thing to suffer loss as an adult, but for me to see my own child overcome with grief, was more than I could handle. It was unbearable, and I could not put her through it again, without her full consent. We moved away from the area a few months later. As soon as we were settled in, my daughter asked if we could start taking foster children again. Of course, we did.

Eight years and several children later, we moved back to the same town where we lived while we took care of little Ronnie. We bought a house and enrolled our adopted third-grader in the local elementary school. Six months later, as I attended an IEP meeting with my son, a tall, thin, blonde-headed boy with big brown eyes, entered the classroom. My heart dropped as I acknowledged eleven-year-old Ronnie! By all indications, he was doing well. My, how he had grown!

Traded Child

Doug was the middle child of five. His two sisters were named after soft drinks. Because there were five children, they had to be placed into three separate foster homes. At the time, we only had space for one boy. Doug was quite a comical little fellow. A slow talking, freckled face kid of eight years, he had been abused by several stepfathers. Most of the men in his mother's life were abusive to her children. This was not his first rodeo. To Doug, it was just a new home to live in for a while.

He was a well-behaved child. He was quiet and played well with others. He did as he was told and never argued. He did have some annoying habits typical for little boys. His most common irritation was that he always stated the obvious. It was harmless and sometimes entertaining. For example, in the middle of a downpour, Doug would say,

"It's raining, huh." Or, "Those are clouds, right."

Once, while sitting at the dinner table with our family, he stated,

"We are going to eat now, huh." Nearly every statement that passed his lips was a declaration. He was fun to talk to even though it was irksome at times.

Doug wet the bed as did many of the children who had been in our care. Most of the children who had been abused had hygiene issues, and would wet the bed as well. I myself wet the bed until I was twelve. I knew firsthand how humiliating it could be. I was very tolerant and found the children were given the responsibility of changing their own bed sheets and taking care of the wet ones, seemed to help them to become less anxious about it. They seemed to feel comfortable, and the bedwetting oftentimes decreased or stopped altogether. The thing that upset me usually, was when they would hide the wet clothes in closets or on top of shoes, or stuffed on top of clean, folded clothing. Doug had done this several times. I put him in charge of the cleanup. His bedwetting decreased, and he no longer hid his wet clothing. He became comfortable enough to take care of his own personal hygiene and tell me when his wet bedding was in the washing machine.

Doug also hoarded food. He seemed to eat plenty at meal times, yet he began hiding food in his dresser, closet, and school backpack. Once, while putting clean clothes in his dresser drawer, I came across a sock full of crackers, cheese and some candy. The sock was carefully lined with toothpicks pointing inward, where they would, and did prick the hands of the finder. His therapist suggested we make Doug aware of snacks that were available for him any time he was hungry. She also informed us that this is merely a learned behavior, necessary for survival for individuals who are not guaranteed their next meal. Having snacks available for him seemed to lessen his hoarding behaviors, but he continued to keep a secret stash of candy and loose change. I let him. It gave him a sense of control. I did not want to take that away from him.

Doug and his siblings had been abused. He had some familiar behaviors that alerted me to watch him closely. Eventually, I had to make a report to his caseworker, and also to his therapist, that he had tried to lure our three-year-old foster child into his bed. This toddler was in our home because he had been molested by his mother. The three-year-old was moved into my bedroom until Doug returned to his own home three weeks later. Six months passed. We received a phone call asking us if we would not only take Doug back permanently, plus one of his sisters. Because of the possibility of adopting the child we had, we decided not to take the children. Evidently, the mother's boyfriend had beaten all five children with a belt, and the judge had given the mother and ultimatum. She had to choose either the boyfriend, or her children. If she chose the children, the boyfriend had to leave her house, and stay gone. If she chose the boyfriend, her parental rights would be terminated and all five of her children would be placed for adoption. She could not have them both. What was her answer?

"I can't live without him," she announced in the courtroom.

I have nothing to add to that.

All in a "Daze" Work

The house was still. The children were all in school for the day. It was early spring. I had just baked cupcakes for an afternoon treat, when I received a phone call from the local police. After a quick greeting, the officer asked if we were still foster parents for the county. I assured him that we were indeed and agreed to take an emergency placement for the day. The officer appeared at our front door a few minutes later, carrying an infant girl in his arms and leading a small army boys, three to be precise. Their names were Harvard, Princeton, and Yale. The baby girl was named Abby. Okay, so I made that up. Actually, one of the little guys was named after a college, and since I cannot recall the other names, I thought I would entertain you.

According to the officer, both of the parents had been arrested on drug charges, and the grandmother could not be located to care for the children. The officer reassured me that they would find her in as soon as possible, and that she would then take them off my hands. No problem. The boys were immediately into everything. It was not long before the baby gates were latched into place. I corralled them into the living room to keep them from being a danger to themselves, and cut back on the cleanup job that was clearly unavoidable. The boys were boisterous and destructive. I quickly put away some of the favorite toys to protect them from breakage. They were equally different to handle and entertain. They were not interested in watching movies or playing games. The baby girl was about eight months old. She was content to sitting on the floor plan with a toy. She did not creep or attempt to crawl. She did not cry or fuss. I wondered if she was simply too terrified to move into the path of one of her brothers. She played quietly on the floor out of the pathway of destruction.

I prepared peanut butter and jelly sandwiches for the boys. They instantly smashed them onto the table and smeared the gooey paste all over the kitchen chairs. They ate a few cheese curls and dump their juice on the floor. When they were finished with lunch, I wondered if they had gotten anything into their tummies. Nevertheless, I gave them a newly frosted cupcake. What in the world was I thinking? Quick as a flash, it was over. Over everything! They somehow managed to stick their feet on the table and smashed the frosting deep into their socks. I never watched an entire lunch explode before. One thing was certain, they were certainly skilled in cupcake demolition.

I cleaned up the kitchen as best I could, and took the boys to the living room to lay them down for a nap. I really needed them to nap because I was tired. I was hopeful. It was easy enough to get them settled on the floor, spaced so they could not touch each other. I sat on the floor in front of the baby and fed her jar of baby food.

I returned to the kitchen to retrieve a bottle of formula. And when I returned, not only were the boys fast asleep, but little Abby had toppled over and was also, sound asleep. I covered her with her little blanket and plopped onto the couch, still holding the warm bottle. I was exhausted, and yet I still needed to tackle the remaining mess and the kitchen. When I finished cleaning, I took advantage of the "cease-fire" and settled in for a quick nap.

My snooze was interrupted by a greatly anticipated phone call. The police had located the grandmother, and they were now on their way to collect the foursome. I tried not to be obviously excited as they gathered the children and their belongings. As they departed, the kind officer thanked me for my time and willingness to babysit for the department. It was then I realized they had never contacted the county office, so I would not be compensated for my time. Chalk one up for community service. I truly served some time that day.

I sighed with great relief the moment the patrol car tail lights disappeared down the street. What an eventful day it had been! I finished my nap with a silly grin on my face. When the kids arrived from school later that afternoon, they asked how my day had been. I did not know where to begin.

"Well." I started. "Everything was pretty normal here, just a regular, uneventful day."

Gabby

Early one spring, during the annual appreciation banquet for foster parents, my husband and I were approached by one of the supervisors. She proposed a simple question.

"How many empty beds do you have?" She inquired.

"Why?" I asked as if I did not already know the answer.

"Well," she replied, "There is his little girl..."

"Say no more"! I interrupted. "When can we see her?" My quick response matched the eagerness that beamed on my husband's face.

"There is more to this," she continued. "She is two years old. Her mother is due in mid-July with her baby sister. Both children will be available for adoption. Are you interested?" She then finished with, "the adoption, it's the real deal!"

Jake and I were thrilled. Not only was a little cherub coming to live with us permanently, but we would soon be getting an angel baby as well. We had hopes of adopting a small sibling group before, but it did not work out, at least, immediately. There were years of struggle and heartbreak as there were ripped from our hearts, and damaged further before they returned to us and their adoption finally materialized. They were teenagers by then. It was worth the pain, in retrospect. The prospects of adopting without a hitch this time, with this sibling group, seemed too good to be true!

With all of this in mind. We made a call to the foster family who was currently caring for Gabby. We made arrangements to visit the following evening to make plans to transfer her to our home. We eagerly waited for the time to meet her. I paused by the empty bedroom and smiled as I imagined Gabby, snuggled up in the pink and purple blankets of the canopy bed. It was a darling bedroom, fit for a princess.

The next evening was full of anticipation. Time passed slowly as we waited it out. Shortly after dinner, we headed for Darlene and Paul's house. In our excitement, we had forgotten to pick up the notepad containing directions to their home. We remembered the street address. How hard could it be? Well. It took us more than an hour to travel what should have taken about fifteen minutes. As we pulled into the foster family's driveway, Jake chuckled with a quick, "We don't want to seem over-anxious now, do we?"

As we climbed the steps to the deck in the backyard, we were greeted by a nervous looking couple. Gabby was playing on the porch with a small kitchen set with play food and dishes. She glanced at me, then offered to bake a cake for me. I joined her at the table and had my cake and ate it too. We chatted back and forth as my husband and the foster parents discussed details of the transfer. Gabby seemed as curious about us as we were about her.

I played longer with Gabby while we finished the soft drinks that were so gratefully provided. I overheard Jake as he asked, "So, when can we pick her up?" My heart was hooked as well. There was just something totally adorable about her. I wanted to take her home with me that evening.

Paul told us that we could take her home with us that evening, but I felt Darlene needed a little more time to adjust. There was something in her eyes that looked a little too familiar. It resembled both relief and sadness. I myself had been there before. It reminded me of how I must have looked when I had made the difficult decision to move a child from her own home. They quickly agreed to have Gabby and things delivered to our home the following evening around six PM.

As our car back of the driveway, I looked at Jake and said, "I feel like we just took a test drive." I wondered what we were getting into. I was concerned as to why this couple had decided not to keep Gabby. Perhaps, they did not want the lifetime commitment that comes with adoption. Maybe, they suspected the cause of the obvious limp in her walk, and the difference in the size of her legs. It did not matter to me what the reason. I was happy to receive this curly haired gift.

The next morning, I adjusted the teddy bears on the canopy bed a dozen times as the day dragged on and on. It seemed as if the clock stopped. My husband paced like an expectant father. After all, was he not? After a long anticipated arrival, our little gift had finally arrived. The red pickup truck backed carefully up to our back door, unloaded two suitcases, one kitchen set, and a small, wide-eyed child.

Ten minutes later, Darlene and Paul were gone. Were left on the porch alone with our new angel. She was content to play with her things, but occasionally looked up and asked, "Where is Darlene?" I reassured her that she was fine, and that she would be staying with us from now on. After a few weeks, she stopped asking. She apparently was quite attached Darlene. She soon transferred her affection to my teen-aged daughter and myself. I learned that she had been passed around, from person to person since her birth. The courts revealed that she had actually only spent a little more than a month with her biological parents.

Two months sped by rather quickly. We enjoyed having Gabby with us as we awaited the birth and placement of her baby sister. The nursery was prepared for her arrival. As baby clothes, diapers, and blankets lay quietly stacked and waiting, we paced. We knew the date of the planned C-section. It was to take place on July fifteenth, the day our newborn would be delivered. We assumed it would take a few days before we would be summoned to the hospital to pick up our newborn angel. We knew it was, as they had promised, a "done deal." It was as exciting as a waiting the birth of one of our own babies.

However, the call never came. We became very anxious and concerned, so we called the county office to check on the baby. There was no explanation given. I was informed rather coldly, that the baby had been born on the fifteenth and was given to an elderly aunt to care for. The parents were homeless and living in their car in the aunts' driveway. They were permitted to care for the baby during the day and would return to their car to sleep at night. It was by far the strangest thing I had ever heard of. Apparently, the aunt did not care much for the couple, but agreed to care for the infant.

The loss was tremendous. I felt very much the way I did when I had miscarried twenty years ago. We went from a baby, to no baby, instantaneously. My heart was wounded so deeply, I felt it would never heal. We were devastated, yet we felt we should have somehow known better. Why did I allow myself to believe so intensely? I had so many questions with no one to ask.

The crib became empty source of pain. It was hard to look at it sitting pretty in the nursery. Jake offered to put it all away for me, but I asked him to wait until our son and his wife came home from the military to visit. They had a brand-new baby, and I wanted her to use the crib. I thought it would help, and it did.

After our son and his family returned home, it was time for me to pick up the pieces and move forward. After spending two weeks doting over my new granddaughter, I did not want to see the crib empty, so Jake packed everything away while Gabby and I played at the park. The summer was over, and I had accepted the fact that Gabby's' little sister would not be coming.

We were aware that there was a noted difference in the size of Gabby's legs. Something did not look quite right, so we made an appointment with an orthopedic doctor. He examined her thoroughly, measuring her from head to toe. After performing series of x-rays, he determined that Gabby might have a genetic disorder. He referred us to a geneticist that later confirmed our fears.

Gabby was diagnosed with Hemi-Hypertrophy, a genetic disorder that cause on side of her little body to grow faster than the other. It was a discrepancy that was more noticeable in her legs and lower body. The doctor explained that Gabby would need to have a test performed every three months until she turned ten years old. I was not sure of the significance of further testing. The doctor explained that Gabby needed to be monitored because the condition caused rapid cell formation, which could lead to the development of tumors growing on major organs.

"Okay now, what are we talking about?" I recall asking.

"Well your daughter may develop tumors." he replied matter-of-factly.

I asked, "What would need to be done if in fact she did develop a tumor?"

He answered, "We would have to operate right way and then choose which type of therapy would be the best for her.

"I'm sorry I started. "What are you talking about?" I began thinking that perhaps I had missed part of the conversation.

"Well if she developed a tumor," he quipped, "it won't be benign."

The room began to spin as I searched through my mind for the meaning of word, 'benign.' Okay, benign is a good thing, wait, he said it would NOT be benign, meaning that it WOULD be cancer!

"What kind of therapy?" I gathered myself then asked calmly.

"We would need to start chemotherapy or radiation treatment as soon as possible.

He assured me that Gabby would be closely monitored every three months, so they could catch it quickly if cancer did develop. He then told me not to worry. He said to follow up with the orthopedic doctor would treat her for the abnormal growth in her right leg. Her pediatrician would prescribe the ultrasounds to be done at the local hospital

Trying to take it all in, I quickly dressed Gabby and walked out into the hallway. My mind was in a whirl. I signaled to my daughter, who was sitting in the waiting room, that we were finished with the doctor. As we walked towards the parking lot, I asked her what seemed to be thousand questions. I felt lost and ready to scream.

"Where did I park the car?" I asked.

"What's wrong?" She asked, as I staggered out the door.

"I will tell you in the car. Where is the car?" She let me by the hand to my little red car.

"Where are my keys?" I continued.

"They are in your hand, mom." She replied with concern in her voice. As I started the car and began to back out of the parking space, I lamented "How in the world do I get out of this stupid parking lot anyway?"

"What's the matter mom?" She inquired again.

"Where do you want to eat? I asked as I pulled into a fast food restaurant.

"This is fine," she answered quietly.

We ordered our meals and took a seat. I told her everything the doctor had said. I tried to explain the seriousness of it, until I saw her expression. She did not look like she was grasping any of the information I was giving to her. I quickly dismissed it and told her that Gabby would be fine and that the doctor would be keeping an eye on her progress. After all, she had not been diagnosed with cancer. I refuse to add "yet". I calmed myself before we headed for home. When I later talk to Jake about the findings, he simply held me and said, "She'll be okay, let's just take this thing one day at a time."

We decided not to stress out about, but instead focus on beautiful angel that the Lord had given us to take care of. She will be tested regularly and we would trust that she would never develop a single tumor.

Gabby was later adopted and never had a sign of a tumor! When she turned ten, we were able to finally stop having the ultrasounds done. She was a happy girl who loved to dance around. She took dance lessons, despite the difference in her legs. We always had a difficult time buying her shoes, since her feet were also different in size. She was always aware of the difference, but it did not seem to bother her. She learned how to stuff tissue in her small foot to keep her shoe from falling off.

Gabby is now thirteen years old. Last year, she had surgery to correct the difference in her leg length, by shortening her right femur bone. The surgeon cut through her right thigh bone, and removed nearly an inch of bone. A plate was added to give her strength as she healed. A few months after surgery, I sat in a lawn chair, as she played field hockey for her school team. It's hard to believe as we look back, how far Gabby has come. We are so thankful that she never developed a single tumor. This would be an entirely different story, if we would have had to add cancer to the equation, a terrible story indeed. We are all so thankful.

Gabby is full of life, and jam-packed of wit. She has a wonderful outlook for her future. When she was five, she told us that she wants to be a pediatric radiologist. She still talks of becoming a doctor, I guess we will see. Gabby the name we gave her, is short for Gabrielle, a beautiful name that will forever remind us that she is in our angel. She's a keeper!

Buddy

I was still going through a period of grief after losing Gabby's baby sister, when I was approached by a caseworker. She stated that she needed to talk to me about something. Uh-Oh. I was reluctant, at first, to follow this lady into her office. Gabby was visiting her family one last time before her adoption would be finalized. I worried that something had come up to maybe stop the adoption. Nevertheless, I followed her. Once in the office, I was a given a chair to sit in as she pulled something from her desk. It looked like a small photo.

"There's this little boy," she began as a braced myself for the worst. "He is thirteen months old, and his parents' rights have already been terminated. He is available for placement and adoption as soon as you give the word."

I sighed in relief and was totally speechless, which is no easy task for me. She told me to take my time, think about it, and talk to my husband. She continued to go on and on about this darling little boy. And then, she handed me the picture.

"Oh, you are not playing fair!" I mused.

"Take your time, no hurry. See what your husband thinks about it, and get back to me." She finished with a Cheshire grin.

"How long have you known Jake?" I asked her.

"Well, nearly twenty years, I guess." She responded.

"Then you already know his answer, don't you?" I chuckled. "I will let you know in a few days. May I keep the picture?" I asked as I close the door behind me. She nodded.

I gathered Gabby and we headed for home. I smiled so hard, my face hurt. I kept thinking of pulling the crib out of storage and setting it up that night. I could barely wait to talk to Jake! As I released Gabby from her car seat, and led her across the street onto the back porch to play with her little kitchen, I motioned for my husband to join me outside. I told him that we needed to talk about something. I told him about the baby, and before I was able to pull his picture of my purse, he asked,

"How soon can we go get him?" As he peered over the photo, I watched his heart melt and run down his cheek.

"As soon as we get back from our vacation." I beamed.

We were to leave early the next morning for a weekend trip. We previously won one of the 'free' stays at a condominium there. It was perfect. Since it was only two hours from my daughter's home, we could be there in time for our granddaughters' birthday.

Early the next morning, we loaded our suitcases into my little red car. Since we were headed south, we stopped for breakfast at a restaurant a few blocks from the county office. Before the waitress refilled my coffee, Jake was on his cell phone. He called to tell our caseworker, Kay, that we definitely wanted the little boy and we would be home the following Monday. He hung up his phone.

"What?" He grinned. "I just wanted to make sure they didn't give him to someone else."

We enjoyed our mini retreat as we playfully scribbled his new name on the hotel stationery. When we went to the class early Saturday morning, we knew full well that we would not be buying a condo. We were only there for the free lunch and the gift card that was promised. We sat through the routine speeches and informational video. We toured the condos and enjoyed the warm weather. When we returned to the classroom, each couple was given a packet that described the many financial options to purchase a 'Time Share'. Our assistant pressed the issue. He was quite the salesman. He nearly convinced us. We desperately needed to be set free from this shark.

Jake told the gentleman that we could not afford to purchase what he was selling. He took the picture of the baby out of his pocket and told him about the pending adoption. He shared how we had previously adopted, and how excited we were to add this child to our family. The words that blurted out of the salesman's mouth made us stand to our feet.

"Why do you need another baby?" He disparaged.

My infuriate husband replied, "Because he needs us!"

The room fell suddenly silent as all eyes were on us. We walked out the door and never looked back. I didn't have the chance to inform the condo agency about the dead rat we found floating in the swimming pool. Rats!

We resumed our little vacation and headed for our daughter's home. We had a good laugh as we shared our experiences. We enjoyed the birthday party at a pizza play land that featured a singing rodent. It was hysterical that when we returned from the party, my son-in-law had a present for my granddaughter. A black rat. Are you kidding me? The irony was too much. I cracked up when I saw it. I hate rats, but for this beautiful little girl's sake, I held it and pretended to like it. I was so creeped out.

We told our daughter about the baby. She was excited for us and very supportive, as all of our children have been through the many years of foster parenting. It was settled. Buddy would become our new son. This was truly a blessing to behold.

I met the baby for the first time, a few days later. He was to spend the weekend with us for a trial visit, mostly to give his foster mother a little time with him before saying the final 'goodbye'. Upon the second visit, which was his actual move to our home, I watched her cuddle and caress the little man who had taken up residence in her heart over the past year. Tears flowed freely as she kissed him and strapped him into the infant seat in my car. His former foster mother had taken care of Buddy for months, as his little body withdrew from the drugs his mother had taken during her pregnancy. This also led to a premature delivery. He weighed only four pounds at birth. As he suffered, she tended to his needs. By the time we met him, his symptoms had decreased markedly. This precious angel was presented to us was an adorable baby boy, who had started out life on the receiving side of his mother's addiction. I know it was difficult for this foster mom to let him go, but she knew she had finished her work.

Buddy was thirteen months old when he came to us. He had a heart defect the doctor said would heal with time. There was no longer a need for monitors or treatment of any kind. His condition required that he be given an antibiotic before having any dental work done. He also had to have minor surgery to correct a urinary problem, but was otherwise healthy. Buddy was not walking yet. He crept around the living room to get around. His smile was awesome. He was such a darling little baby. He was content and happy as long as the house was calm. Sudden noises made him stressed. He would cry until things were calm again. At night, he wrestled around and screamed on a regular basis. We started off with his crib in our bedroom, so he would not disturb the whole household. He would cry out at least three times in the night. At first, I tried to rub his back to help him go back to sleep. However, I soon realized I was irritating him more. We began ignoring his brief cry until he would soothe himself back to sleep. This worked well, yet, it disrupted our sleep. We soon moved his crib to the living room where we could play music featured on the cable station. He appeared to like classical music the most. This seemed to help. We began taking turns sleeping on the couch, so one of us could be near him. It was a good plan. It was not the best solution, however, we did this for the better part of a year.

When our older son turned eighteen and moved out, we quickly took over his small bedroom for Buddy. When our son left, it was not on the best of terms. Remodeling was therapeutic and a great stress relief. The carpet was laid on the fourth day, and the bed was put together shortly after. When our son came home to apologize for his behavior he was quite surprised to see how quickly his room had changed.

"Does this mean I can't come back home?" He asked.

"There is a couch in the basement," I answered, with a laugh.

Teddy loved his new bedroom. It was decorated with his two favorite things, sports and teddy bears. We bought him a CD player and some Christian children's music. We set it to continually play. This has helped him tremendously with his sleep. When he cried out, the music soothed him, and he would quickly fall back to sleep. He seemed more rested in the morning. He still gets stressed out now and then, but mostly when he gets overly tired.

Buddy is quite a charmer. He is a real treasure that we have found. He is biracial, as is his big sister, Gabby. Although they are not blood related, they look like biological siblings. He was a handsome little fellow with long locks of hair that I used to keep braided in cornrows. His heritage is important to us, and we intend to celebrate our differences.

He has grown into such a nice young man of twelve. He is a hard worker who loves to help out around the house, or to do anything with his dad. He does not have any learning disabilities. He doesn't like homework, but who does? He wears his hair short now and is quite handsome. I will forever cherish the day we met.

God's timing is impeccable. Although I do not fully understand why we were passed over for the Gabby's baby sister, I accept it. It still amazes me that only one month later we were given this beautiful boy to keep. It was an awesome experience, and I cannot for a moment, grasp it. We simply cannot imagine our life without Buddy. He is a real treasure.

I admit I was more than curious about the little sister who was now eleven years old. I have never seen her. I surely believe that each child is placed in our home for a purpose, no matter how long or how brief. Each one is determined by God. I will not question his ways.

Smoldering Angel

A five-year-old burn victim was to be released into our custody. She needed to be placed in a clean home where she could be safe and hygienic, due to her severe injury. I took it as a compliment when the agency chose my home. I dropped by the county office on my way home from work. It was there I would meet Lisa.

My initial reaction to seeing Lisa was one of shock and horror. I had never seen anyone burned so badly. Even now, it brings a gasp to my lips and a tear to my eye. How could this have happened to such a little girl? Her face was blistered along her cheeks and chin from ear to ear. The skin on her chest was thick and marred from the skin grafts. There were large holes in between the grafts that formed oozing crevices. Her face was red and swollen. Her nose was not burned at all, but her chin and cheek area resembled a five o'clock shadow. I am not trying to be funny here, but this is the only description I could think of, as far as the extent of burns on her little face.

Lisa had been visiting her aunt's home when she decided to play with a lit candle. She put her shirt over the flame. The shirt caught fire and she was engulfed in the flames. Her aunt panicked and pulled Lisa's enflamed shirt up over her head, causing her to inhale flames which burned her esophagus. The shirt burned into Lisa's chest, causing the third degree burns. The burned flesh had to be surgically removed as Lisa fought for her life. She was put in an induced coma for three months while they grafted skin they had removed from her thighs, to attach to her chest. The story alone, is a nightmare. Nevertheless, I agreed to take her home with me.

Lisa ran wildly around the corridor as we waited, impatiently for the elevator. Her short haircut made her look like a little boy. I presumed her hair had been badly burned. I learned that her head was shaved while she was in the hospital, recovering from the trauma of the burns. Apparently, she once had long, blonde hair deeply infested with head lice. Her pretty green dress identified her as a girl.

Lisa seemed as if she hadn't a care in the world. Most children are at least a little apprehensive about meeting strangers, especially when they are being removed from their own home. Lisa jumped into my car and began playing with the little stuffed animals in the back seat.

As we travelled together, I couldn't help but peek at her through the rear view mirror. Each time I glanced, I cringed. As we arrived home, my two little ones met us at the door. I had previously warned the children of Lisa's appearance and asked them to be kind, and not to be afraid of what they would see. They were polite and empathetic. They immediately took Lisa to the play room. At the dinner table, I lost my appetite. Lisa lacked in table manners and the sight of food on her facial burns made me sick to my stomach. My heart ached as I wanted to take away her pain. I wasn't prepared for bath time. I had to use surgical soap to cleanse her wounds. I was totally unprepared for what I was about to see.

Lisa's chest and upper arms had been brutally charred, suffering third degree burns. Second degree burns covered her from her lower chest to her navel. As I removed the sterile bandages, I noticed she was still forming blisters on the tender parts of her skin. I asked my firefighter son why she would blister like that.

"Her own body temperature is continuing to burn her where it is most tender." He replied. I needed a moment.

Lisa requested a cool bath because warm water made her burn. I accommodated her. My four-year-old daughter asked if she could bathe with Lisa. She did not want Lisa to be afraid. I smiled as Gabby shivered in the tub with her new friend. It was a scene of innocence and true compassion. I choked up as I reached for the sponge. Lisa answered Gabby's questions as I gently cleaned the burned areas. After patting her dry, I applied burn cream and bandaged her chest and arms. She also had to wear an arm brace that would keep her arm from touching her side. If her arms touched her side, there was a possibility that her underarm wound would bond to her arm and she would not have full use of her arm. As is was, there was a 'web' under her arm that needed to eventually be stretched.

After tucking the girls into bed and kissing them on the forehead, I went to my bedroom and closed the door behind me. There I sobbed uncontrollably, and cried, "I cannot do this!" After some time and plenty of tears, I resigned to the fact that this little girl needed me to be strong, for her.

Over the summer months, her wounds were healed enough for me to start therapy. Three times a day I would lay her on the coffee table and apply yet another cream to her scarred, little body. I kneaded her little chest and stretched her bad arm as far as she could tolerate, rubbing the cream deep into her skin. I would work with her for about an hour each time. It was physically exhausting as well as emotionally draining.

Like many other children we housed, Lisa was a hoarder. She began displaying other bizarre behaviors as well. She began taking things from people and placing the items in Gabby's dresser drawer. She started smearing toothpaste and lotion into her hair. She would squat on the carpet and urinate. She would have bowel movements on the floor as well. She would then roll them into little balls, and place them in Gabby's bed or dresser. She seemed to obsess over meals and began overeating and hoarding food in her dresser. She was rapidly gaining an unhealthy weight.

I cried often for Lisa. Things were getting out of control and I began to worry about the safety of my other children. There was a daily escapade. It seemed I was constantly met with new issues to deal with. The care for her burns, coupled with behavior problems, began to take a toll on the family, as well as my nerves. I recruited my older daughter to come and help me with Lisa's treatments. I needed a break. I was at the end of my rope and there were no more knots to cling to.

After three more months of turmoil, we painfully decided to have her moved to a therapeutic foster home, where she could get some desperately needed one-on-one care. The agency found a placement for Lisa two weeks before Christmas. Her gifts were all wrapped and placed into boxes so she could enjoy her presents from us. Her belongings were returned to her suitcases, and she was on her way. She jumped into the caseworker's car, and began to smile and wave goodbye. She had not bonded with our family, so to her, she was just on another adventure. I sighed with bittersweet relief as the car disappeared from sight.

I know that I did all I could do for Lisa. It was the most difficult case we had ever had. I don't know where she is now, or how much she has healed. I only know that for a time, she lived in our home, but she will forever live in my heart.

P.J. and Smiley

We moved into the country and decided that we no longer wanted to be foster parents. How many times have I said that before? I have no idea. We decided that we wanted to see if we could adopt a small boy and girl. Since Gabby and Buddy were the only children who were in our home, we thought, "Why not?"

I made a few calls to the county office, and within a few weeks, our home study was completed. We were given information on adoption through the foster care program. We also acquired a web address that contained pictures and information on children across the nation who were waiting to be adopted. I registered on line and began to search. Daily, I scrolled through the list of prospects. I was in search of a brother and sister sibling group between the ages of four and six, the ages of my two children. When I found a sibling set that met the requirements, I would then make an inquiry, and leave my contact information.

In the six months that followed, I had become discouraged. This was harder than I thought. I had made twenty-three enquiries without a single response. Then, two days before Christmas, I received a phone call. It's hard to believe how many things have happened around this holiday.

"Hello?" I said as I picked up the phone.

"Is this Andela?" asked the lady on the other end of the line.

"Yes it is!" I replied. I sensed a bit of excitement in her voice.

"I think we found your kiddos!" she exclaimed.

She informed me that a caseworker in a faraway state, had reviewed our family profile on the adoption site I had registered on, six months prior. She asked if we would mind getting a call from the children's caseworker. I could not wait for the call! Minutes later, the phone rang again. Of course, I grabbed it up rather quickly. It was decided. We talked for over an hour. We began making plans to fly that February, to meet the African American children who would soon become a part of our colorful family.

Christmas was exciting as Gabby and Buddy were eager to get a new brother and sister. It was awesome that, this time, we would not have to give them back. It was also scary. I rationalized that by this point, I had dealt with over a hundred different children in my home over the past twenty-something years. I was worn with experience.

Time seemed to drag on. Suddenly, we found ourselves in a jetliner. Upon arriving at the airport, we were directly met by the young caseworker from the county. She filled us in on the plans for the weekend and paused long enough to ask if we had any questions. Surprisingly, I was speechless. I had nothing to say. I think I was absorbing so much information that my brain froze.

We checked into our motel room to freshen up before dinner. The young caseworker planned to pick us up and take us to the children's foster home, where we could meet them, before we went out for pizza. It was overwhelming, to be honest. There were five other children in the home. No one checked the children's behaviors at the restaurant. We were loud and busy at our table. Our two seemed curious and nervous at the same time. The little girl grinned constantly, and her brother played with my hair. He had no problem getting close. His sister was more reserved.

After dinner, and the return to the home, the kiddos, retrieved a small bag from their bedroom. They were excited to return to the motel with us to spend the weekend. Over the next two days, we swam and played. We made a trip to take in the sites. It was a beautiful, crispy, clear day. The sun shined bright as we were able to get some amazing snapshots. It was a wonderful time of bonding together. I asked the children if they wanted to keep their birth names, or if they wanted to choose something else. The little girl blurted out what she wanted to be called. Her brother exclaimed, "Jack Black! I want to be called, Jack Black!" We laughed hysterically. He thought for a while and said, "Actually, how about P.J. And so it was decided.

The plan was then, that the children would be flown to us at the end of March. I felt sad that we would be leaving them for another month. It seemed we were leaving our children behind. We had bonded nicely, even though Smiley was slightly apprehensive.

March 30th would have been my mother's birthday. We lost her to cancer and heart disease, only months before. On the way to the airport, to pick the children and their caseworker, I couldn't help but smile. Mom would have loved these kids. To bring them home on her birthday, caused a hot tear to run down my cheek.

The house rang with excitement as we settled the children in. There was an immediate connection as the children played together. We had a party at the church to introduce the newcomers to the congregation, as well as our family. Soon, it was time for our new friend to fly back. She smiled as she entered the terminal, knowing the children finally had a forever family.

As time went on, we began to pick up on some survival behaviors that have lessened or completely diminished over the last five years. There were hoarding issues, along with stealing and lying. It was exhausting to be constantly on the lookout for a crime. Constant supervision was necessary. Some of the 'victims' were less than forgiving. I found myself wondering if we would ever be able to trust P.J. at all. Many times, I became overwhelmed with frustration, and kept him home from church, because I did not want to face the looks he received from some of the congregation.

He is now doing well, with a few offences here and there. We simply deal with the problem, and move on. He has a learning disability, and has Attention Deficit Hyperactive Disorder, and is currently treated with medication. He is a loving, comical clown. When he is not frustrating us, he is making us laugh. He is adorable. I'm glad he is our son. He is now twelve years old.

Smiley is now eleven years old. She does well in school, and is active in sports. She still grins and loves to be treated like a princess. She has a head full of hair that I often struggle with. She is a beautiful soul. She loves to be dressed up pretty. She also is A.D.H.D. with O.D.D. (Oppositional Defiance Disorder) and treated with medication. I cannot imagine what it would be like without these two kiddos in my life. I'm thankful that God brought them into our home, in His time.

Mare-Mare

A month after we relocated to another state, I decided that we had an uneven number of children that must be remedied. Since there were a total of six boys who bore the Jamison name, and only five girls, I needed another girl. I got the home study and began my search for a four-year-old girl. They are awesome at that age. I found no one to fit the bill. Smiley claimed that she was the baby and wanted it to remain that way.

Late November, we received the call. A ginger-haired angel needed a permanent home. She was thirteen. I was anxious to meet her and within a few hours, she was delivered to our door. She was shy and reserved. Gabby showed her to her room as we discussed the details with her caseworker. I cannot get into details, since this is still too fresh.

Six months later, Mare's adoption was finalized. This was the first time that a biological mother was invited to the adoption proceedings. She was a nice lady who had to make a painful decision. She decided what was best for her children. Mare had two siblings who had been adopted by their grandparents.

I was given a bouquet of roses when I entered the courtroom. It was only natural for me to give Mare's mother a single rose. I wanted it to symbolize the bond between us. We had a daughter in common. Nothing was ever going to change that. It was emotional for her, but she knew her daughter would be well cared for. I have to say that that particular adoption was different than any of the others. It was beautiful, and satisfying.

Mare has continued her relationship with her mother. She had blended into our family so smoothly, that I knew it was from the Lord. She is a beautiful, bright teenager now armed with her learner's permit. Her dad takes her driving, since I am a coward. She consistently makes the honor roll in school. She takes several advanced classes. Mare loves cheerleading and hanging out with her boyfriend. She is a computer whiz and has helped me out of many a pickle.

I only accepted two other placements since the move. One fourteen-year-old young lady was quite inappropriate with my teen girls, and was promptly removed after a physical altercation, and subsequent abuse report. My girls did not feel safe.

Another, younger girl stayed with us for a month. She was an adorable eight-year old. She shared a bedroom with Smiley. She was fine until something set her off, and then she would physically tear into poor Smiley, punching, kicking and swearing at her until we would, quite literally, have to pull her off. We tried everything we could think of to keep Smiley safe, all the while, she insisted that she was okay, and begged us to let Abby stay.

After a while it was quite clear that we could no longer keep Abby. It broke my heart to see how violent she had become. I called the agency, once, twice, three times to no avail. They seemed to offer no solutions, but excuses, as to why they could not remove her. In desperation, I attended a planning session for Abby, with a letter of resignation in my hand. I listened as they tried to pressure me into keeping her even longer.

"Look," I said. "It would be one thing if Abby was thrashing at me or my husband. I could tolerate that. But, to see her blacken our little girl's eye or scratch her face, that is completely unacceptable!"

"We understand your concerns, Mrs. Jamison, why don't you give it a little more time?' came the answer.

"Here is my letter of resignation." I protested. "I am no longer a foster parent."

The meeting finished as we made plans for Abby's extraction. Within the next twenty-four hours, she was promptly removed from our home. It was sad, once again, for me to have to ask for a child to be moved, especially in this manner. This would be the end of my career as a foster parent.

I am glad that Mare-Mare was our final adoption. It seems right. I have a dozen children. Six boys and six girls. Five currently reside in our home. The others have since married and have given me fifteen grandchildren. After twenty-five years of foster parenting, I have fought a good fight, I have finished my course.

Conclusion

How can you give them up? Sometimes, I think that if I heard that question one more time, I will throw up. For as long as we have been foster parents, someone has been sure to come up with this query. If I had a nickel every time we were asked that question. Oh, I can be rather sarcastic at times, and, believe me, I have answered quite sharply at times. Once, I simply replied, oh, it's easy to give them up. I just rip my heart out of my chest and pack it with their underwear!

I never wanted anyone to feel sorry for us as the children would come and go. I didn't know how to make people understand that losing them was part of the big picture. If they had never been a part of our lives, we could not have helped them. It would have been selfish of us to have been more concerned with their own feelings, then those of the children with whom we shared our home. It is painful, but we have learned to accept the pain as part of the cure. Of course, as I have shared my feelings regarding loss. I hope I have also shared the joys of adoption.

I want to caution those who would like to become foster parents; unless you really feel a call on your life, and love children, I would not recommend it. It is a painful pill to take. I have seen many foster parents who seemed uncaring, and provided nothing more than custodial care. All the needs were met, but they did not get emotionally involved. I believe the children deserve more than simply being physically taken care of.

I have been struggling for an appropriate ending to this book, and I could not find one. My sister-in-law once asked if we were crazy to take in more children. I answered, I don't think so. I shared this with my husband, who laughed and said, "I don't know. Would we know if we were crazy?"

Sometimes, I wonder how much of a difference we had actually made in the lives of children. There have been some joyous occasions the Jamison household since we became foster/adoptive parents. There have been equally as many tearful departures. Has it all been worth it? How can one truly measure one's investment in the life of the child? It cannot be done. We have surely been enriched by our experiences, and are blessed to have been able to adopt eight children. But, I wondered how we affected the children.

I kept a letter I had received in the mail. As I was searching for the perfect ending for this book, I came across it. It was from our daughter who had been previously adopted. She had moved out of our home as soon as she turned eighteen. She was not happy with us when she left. The letter came to us a month later, simply addressed, 'Mom and Dad', followed by our home address.

"Mom and Dad,
I just wanted to take this time to tell you how much I appreciate you! Thank you so much for everything you have done for me. I enjoyed having lunch with you the other day. Sorry, I did not really talk that much. I love spending time with you! I know the last month was hard for everyone, and I'm really sorry for everything. I just want you to know that I was never mad at either of you. Basically, I was just trying to be grown, but I'm glad everything is okay now. One thing that has been on my mind, is that I hope you don't feel like I neglect you when I go visit my mom. I just want you to know that I don't choose my real mom over you. It's just that sometimes I feel that I am the only one my mom has.

You guys should know that. Thank you Mom and Dad. I miss you and love you all.

Love, Terri"

We have received very few letters from children who have been in our care. Once, we got a note from a woman who thanked us for taking care of her son for a year. Things were better at home, and she was grateful for the love we had shown her son. He was turning out to be a nice young man, and she thanked us for making a difference in his life.

Another former foster child wrote to inform us that he was going into the military, and wanted us to know how much he appreciated what we had done for him.

I heard from a young friend of one of our first foster children, that she was married and had two children. She told us that the young woman often spoke of our kindness.

It was always painful when the children that we loved and lived with for a while were returned to their families. We cried, we grieved, and got on with our lives. I find it is better to have loved and lost than to have never loved. I have repeated that phrase again and again over the past quarter of a century. It has never failed to give me comfort, and the courage to love again. If I did not love children enough to suffer for them, I would not have made a very good foster parent. Unless you can walk in my soggy moccasins, you will never understand how it works. If you are called by God to do something, he will give you all the grace need to succeed in your walk. It is not a mystery, it's called LOVE.

"END"